BOOKS BY MAURICE GROSSER

The Painter's Eye

Critic's Eye

Painting in Our Time
(originally *Painting in Public*)

PAINTER'S

PROGRESS

MAURICE GROSSER

Clarkson N. Potter, Inc./Publisher   NEW YORK
DISTRIBUTED BY CROWN PUBLISHERS, INC

FIRST EDITION
Library of Congress Catalog Card Number: 70-169048
Printed in the United States of America
Published simultaneously in Canada
by General Publishing Company Limited.
DESIGN: MARGERY KRONENGOLD

ACKNOWLEDGMENTS

I have many friends to thank for help and information; in particular, Dr. Robert Lewis, Mr. Hugh Carton, Mr. Desmond Kingsley, Mr. Robert Hatch of the *Nation* and Mr. Donald Richie of the Museum of Modern Art of New York for their great help on the manuscript and proofs; the physicists Mrs. Hans Jaffe and Mr. Allen Holden, Dr. Charles R. Rubenstein and Dr. Donald E. Person of the Bell Laboratories and Dr. W. C. Huckle of Hercules Inc.; Mr. Frederick Hartt of the University of Virginia, Mr. Jonathan Mayne of the Victoria and Albert Museum, Mr. Harry Greer of the Frick Collection, Professor Henry-Russell Hitchcock, Mr. Robert H. Rosenblum, and the librarians of the Frick Collection and of the Metropolitan Museum for their help in assembling the illustrations.

To my friend Virgil Thomson
A gift for his birthday

CONTENTS

· 1 ·

DRAWING

AND LEARNING

TO DRAW

THERE HAS NOT been anybody in my time to whom one could go to learn to paint. The art schools of my youth were good enough at teaching drawing, but they were not at all good in the other branches of professional knowledge, like the techniques of oil painting, or the use of color, or how to compose a picture. The successful professional painters who knew about such things had long ceased the practice of taking pupils into their ateliers as they had formerly done. One was forced to pick up what one could and piece it together. Now, as a way of passing on what I have been able to find out, I am setting out here to tell what little I know about the practice of the art, how and where I learned it, and which parts I think will work and which will not. Perhaps the best way to begin is with how I myself happened to become a painter.

It was in the fall of 1921. I was a sophomore at Harvard. A friend of my roommate's came into our study at Matthews Hall, visibly pleased and excited. He had been to a life class at the Boston Architectural School and was going again.

"You can see a naked woman for a quarter," he said to me. "Why don't you come along?" "I don't know how to draw," I remember saying. "You don't need to," he said. "I don't either. You just pretend to be an art student. Most of them don't know how to draw anyway." So I went.

The class was held at night in a basement room of a building on Commonwealth Avenue. It had already begun. The model, to our disappointment, was not a naked woman but a plump young man in a jockstrap. He was posed on a platform raised a foot or so from the floor. A strong light from above cut his body into a pattern of sharply divided lights and shadows. The students stood around him at their easels, drawing in charcoal on large pieces of white paper. Those nearest the platform were seated, their drawing boards propped on chairs in front of them. With the glaring overhead lights and the corners of the room in shadow, it made a scene very like the nineteenth-century life-classes one finds in paintings of the times.

The class was primarily for architectural students, to teach them enough freehand drawing to enable them to furnish their architectural renderings with trees and figures. There were a half dozen of these, serious young men doing neat and stylized work. There were also a handful of younger people, students from the nearby art schools getting in some extra practice in figure drawing, and along with these, seven or eight of those devoted amateurs always to be found in classes of this sort; ladies and gentlemen who had taken up painting as a hobby late in life and whose drawings always presented the identical image—the rubbery outline of a body provided with a set of timid ideograms to indicate hair, features, fingers, breasts, and navel, each carefully assigned to its expected place. No one in the class was very good. There was not even an instructor; one of the older students was in charge. I paid my twenty-five-cents admission, bought a piece of paper, a stick of charcoal, and an eraser, found for myself an easel and a drawing board, set them up in a place where I could see the model, and began. I believe my companion did the same; my recollection of this is no longer clear. His expectations having been deceived, he may have left. At any rate, he stepped out of the picture, and I do not remember seeing him again till he appeared more than four decades later at the opening of a show of mine.

I do remember, however, the drawing I made, and that it was not big enough. I had placed my figure in the middle of the paper with room to spare on every side, whereas the figures drawn by all the experienced students took up the whole sheet. I do not see how my drawing could possibly have been any good, but I seem to remember that it was as good as any of the others. It may well have been.

At any rate, I was enormously pleased and not a little astonished. It was my younger brother, not I, who was believed to be the artist in our family, and who, as a child, had copied characters from comic strips and pretty girls from magazine covers. I was only an insatiable reader; my bent was supposed to be literary. I had gone to a school in Middle Tennessee, founded and run by a Civil War veteran, with a course of study straight out of the eighteenth-century English public schools—Greek, Latin, and mathematics, and no other subjects whatsoever, not even history or geography except what was needed as background for the Greek and Latin writers. At Harvard, I was majoring in mathematics, not that I had any special talent for it, but because I had been well grounded in it and found it easy.

None of this had prepared me for the delights of freehand drawing. Here was quite another order of reality—not a passive acquaintance with things other people had said and done, but a hand-to-hand encounter with the outside world. I had found my calling, and though I continued my courses in mathematics, and even graduated with honors in the subject, my real interest henceforth was painting.

From that time on, as long as I remained at Cambridge, I attended life classes five times a week—on Tuesdays and Thursdays at the Architectural School, and at the South Boston Art School on the other week-day nights. The latter, being held at a real art school, were the more serious, with an accomplished draftsman as instructor and students who drew very well. The routine of both classes was the same. And since drawing from the nude has had such importance in art teaching of the past—ever so much more than today—I might as well describe it in detail.

The paper one drew on was of standard size—a twenty-five by nineteen inch sheet of thin, laid, rag paper, usually made in France and bearing the evocative trade names of Ingres and Canson-Mongolfier (the same Mongolfiers who made the first balloon, and that in paper too). The figure had to be drawn large enough to fill the entire sheet, no matter how far away from the model one stood to work, the head of the figure being placed at the top of the sheet and the feet at the bottom. One usually drew in charcoal because it is so easy to erase. Anything that cannot be dusted off the paper with a piece of chamois can be lifted out with the point of a kneaded rubber. Besides, in charcoal, gradations of tone are easy to achieve simply by smearing with a finger. When the drawing was finished, one fixed it by spraying it with a thin solution of shellac.

Charcoal, nevertheless, is not a medium with much natural charm. It can be erased and changed indefinitely—that is its value to students—but overerasure and damp fingers only too quickly rob the paper of its bloom, and the dark tones grow blotched and dirty. Remembering this, one is always astonished by the beauty of tone and texture of Sargent's charcoal studies (Fig. 1). But his was not student's work. His lines and smudges were put down with an assured hand. Nothing ever needed changing, and the surface of the paper was never disturbed.

A more attractive drawing medium is Conté crayon, or red chalk, and this we sometimes used. It comes in square sticks of three colors, brick-red, brown, and black. Red chalk never seems to get as heavy and dirty as charcoal, perhaps on account of the agreeable color of its lines and shadings. But the sticks are waxy, not dry like charcoal, and much more difficult to erase. Red chalk was the favorite drawing medium of Watteau and the other sixteenth- and seventeenth-century masters. If one wished, one could imitate their methods by working with red chalk on tinted paper and then picking out the highlights with white chalk. But this we seldom practiced. It led to the making of pretty drawings for their own sake and away from the sober exercise of seeing form and putting it down, which was the real purpose of these classes.

Anyone who has not studied drawing cannot possibly imagine how simple are the means by which a drawing is set up. They are nothing but commonplace little tricks for comparing shapes and measuring proportions. One learns to hold up a stick of charcoal at arm's length from the eye, to mark off on it with the point of one's thumb the apparent height of the model's head, and then to use this measure as a unit to establish on one's paper the general proportions of the model's body—so many heads from head to foot, so many heads from foot to groin, from groin to navel, from crotch to chin. One learns to hold the stick at an angle to connect the model's salient points and, sighting along it, to check the slope from shoulder to elbow, from knee to wrist, and so on, and thus to establish a web of imaginary lines enclosing the figure and further verifying the proportions. One is shown how to make use of a plumb line to check the verticals and get the figure properly balanced on its feet. "Positions and measures" all this was called. Once the proportions were established and the figure set up with its outline roughly drawn, one began to work in the lights and shadows, trying by means of these to express the body's solid mass. The lighting in these classes was invariably harsh, with impenetrable shadows on the unlit part of the figure, as in Ribera or Caravaggio. The forms of the knee of a standing figure, almost always in shadow, were difficult to make out, and the neck under the chin impossible. It was years before I learned to draw them properly.

4

Fig. 1. JOHN SARGENT, charcoal study of Robert Harrison, Jr., circa 1920s.
Collection Mr. and Mrs. John Koch.

The method of drawing favored at the South Boston School—I never encountered it elsewhere—was first to establish the outline of the figure, and then within this to map out the areas of shadow, making their boundary lines smudged or sharp to follow where the shadow terminal on the model herself was gradual and where it was abrupt. One then filled in the shadow side with a uniform tone, or even left it in white paper if one wished. To further this simplification into two basic tones, almost no shading was permitted us in the lighted parts. The result, nevertheless, was a quite surprising effect of solid form—that is if the student had been able to see and understand the model's solid forms to begin with. It was a trick, of course, depending on a completely artificial stage-light setup. But it simplified everything and made for professional-looking drawings. Actually, an artificial restriction such as this is very useful in instruction. It is so arbitrary, so contrary to experience, that the student is forced into revolt, and in trying to circumvent the limitation, finds out for himself things he would otherwise never have discovered. And the trick itself does not become too dangerous a mannerism as long as one remembers that this accidental array of shadows, which changes with every movement of the model, has no significance, and that what we are attempting to record is the permanent structure underneath, the solid, sculptural forms of limb and torso on which the shadows lie. And this is a general rule in drawing: No matter in what manner or style the drawing is made—in line, in shapes of black and white, in full chiaroscuro, in flat silhouette, in balloon-like rotundities—the drawing is successful, and informative, in direct proportion to how well the draftsman has understood the solid forms in front of him. Compare the drawings of Degas (Figs. 2, 3) and Matisse (Figs. 4, 5) and then compare their sculpture, and you will see what I mean. It is evident from the sculpture alone, though the drawings confirm it, that Degas' knowledge of form was profound and that Matisse's was hasty and relatively superficial.

Practice such as this, drawing from the nude as a basic training for beginners, is the most venerable tradition of the painting profession. The name itself for the kind of drawings we made points this out. The nude done in charcoal as a school exercise is called an "academy," and is almost the only trace left in the world today of the academic system of art instruction, invented in the sixteenth century, which formed European painters and dominated Western painting for almost three hundred years.

During the Middle Ages, painting instruction was the province of the guilds. Even in Renaissance times, when painting had at length acquired the status of an art, it was still taught as a craft and practiced as a trade. If a young man wished to become a painter, he entered a master's workshop as an apprentice. He was a servant and received wages. More likely than not, he was confined to the premises night and day for fear that he might betray the secrets which were his master's most valuable stock-in-trade. There exists in Auvergne today a paper mill dating from those times, where paper is still made by the old hand methods in the original buildings, and where one can still see the shuttered, mattressed cupboards in which the youngsters were bolted up at night for just this caution- ary reason—because they knew the secrets. In circumstances such as these, the apprentice learned to imitate his master's style and to paint indistinguishably on his master's pictures; individuality was not the prerogative of the individual but of the shop. An apprentice he remained until he had painted his masterpiece, "masterpiece" being an original picture sufficiently skillful to fulfill guild require- ments. He could then become a guild member and set up a shop of his own. The guild saw to it that standards of workmanship were respected and that the tradi- tional knowledge of the craft was preserved. And if the guild was not the final authority on taste—the client has always been that—it was nevertheless the final and legally recognized authority on artistry and workmanship.

The Carracci family, Agostino, Annibale, and Lodovico, changed all this. In a school they established in Bologna in 1585, called the Academy on account of the name's classical associations, they began to teach painting on a more liberal system. Here the beginner was no longer an apprentice; he was a student, not an employee; he paid tuition. He was an independent man who could afford to cultivate his originality. His training consisted of two disciplines: of drawing from the antique and from the nude, and of copying pictures by recognized mas- ters. Drawing, because pictures at that time were not painted from life or from nature, but from drawings the painter had already made. And copying pictures, because if one is not working directly with the man who painted the picture, copying it is the only way to discover how its particular effects of paint have been obtained. Thus, unlike the guilds, the academic system made available to the student a great variety of painting styles. Just the same, it had its disadvantages. There was no provision, as there had been in the guilds, for the handing down of trade secrets from master to apprentice, so that the precise and tested information about painting methods, about recipes, materials, and handling, which the guilds had so carefully safeguarded, began from this moment on to get lost. Painters who taught at the academies could pass on their methods; those who did not could not. The academies themselves had very little place for trade secrets. They taught a more readily available knowledge, the basic things which everyone in

Fig. 2. DEGAS, Woman Bathing in a Shallow Tub, 1885. Pastel on paper.
The Metropolitan Museum of Art. The H. O. Havemeyer Collection.
Bequest of Mrs. H. O. Havemeyer, 1929.

Fig. 3. DEGAS, The Tub. Cast in bronze in 1920 by Hebrard after Degas's death.
The Metropolitan Museum of Art. The H. O. Havemeyer Collection.
Bequest of Mrs. H. O. Havemeyer.

Fig. 4. HENRI MATISSE, Nude Study, circa 1910. Pen and ink.
Collection, *The Museum of Modern Art, New York. Purchase.*

Fig. 5. HENRI MATISSE, The Back, III, circa 1914 (?). Bronze. *Collection, The Museum of Modern Art, New York. Mrs. Simon Guggenheim Fund.*

---

the profession knew, and which, in the long run, reduces to what happens to get written down in books. This is why there is so little usable information left today about the techniques of the pre-Academic painters such as van Eyck or Tintoretto, and even of many of the later painters as well. How these painters worked and what they used did not get written down, or if it did, has not come down to us in any form that we can interpret and use.

Throughout the seventeenth and eighteenth centuries, academies built on the Bologna model flourished. Beginning as painting schools with well-known painters as instructors, they developed into associations of successful artists which, as well as being in charge of art education, also provided exhibitions where members' work was shown. As professional bodies, they jealously maintained their authority in matters of taste, artistic quality and prices. In the nineteenth century they fell into disrepute. The Realists of the fifties disowned them. The Impressionist revolt of the seventies finished them off. In fact, they were so discredited that by the beginning of our century, the word *academic* had become the final and damning term of abuse for a work of art. For three full centuries, the academies and their teaching had furnished the framework for all Western painting, from the allegories of Poussin and the battle pictures of Salvator Rosa down to the ungainly historical compositions still being annually run up at the Ecole des Beaux-Arts by students competing for the Prix de Rome. But in the twenties, when I was beginning my studies, all that remained of this complex body of tradition was the habit of drawing from the nude in charcoal on a large piece of paper.

And this was about all that could be got at the art schools of the twenties. They offered little else. All the rest of the academies' traditions, aimed at teaching how to paint a large picture in the studio—how to plan and compose the picture from sketches, how to enlarge the sketches on to canvas, how to begin with an underpainting in which all the modeling and the lights and shadows were executed in monochrome after drawings done from nature, and how to complete the whole in color, using color notes as well as live models and real objects brought into the studio—all this had vanished. Vanished also were the ateliers like that of Carolus-Duran which had followed the Manet-Velázquez tradition, where one could learn to construct large pictures by direct painting from the model, and which had turned out all the great brush-virtuosos of the beginning of our century like Zorn and Sorolla and Sargent—none of these ateliers existed, not even in Paris. At any art school of the time, a student could still learn how to draw the figure. But there was no one to teach him how to relate the figure to a background, or to paint it in color, or to fill the space in his canvas with air and depth, or even how to compose a picture. This, in a way, was the exact opposite of the art schools of today, where the student learns to construct a picture but is not taught how to draw from nature.

Consequently, in the Paris of the twenties, all art schools were discredited. No practicing artist took them seriously, and students learned to paint, and even to draw, not from the art schools, but by association with their elders and their fellows. In America and in England, where the schools still retained some authority, the graduates came out excellent draftsmen. But they were obliged to find out for themselves how to go about painting a picture. And although I did not yet know it, this was already the path I was set on—the search for some sort of painting tradition I could use.

· 2 ·

WATERCOLORS
IMPRESSIONISM
AT HARVARD

THE ART DEPARTMENT at Harvard, when I was there, was in no way an art school. That is to say, it had no interest in turning out professional painters. But it was very interested indeed in turning out people for museum work. The old Fogg Museum, which was the seat of the art department, was run by top men in the museum and art-scholarship field: Arthur Sachs, Edward Forbes, Chandler Post, who professed both Greek literature and Spanish painting, Arthur Pope, and Kingsley Porter. And here, in my time, were trained all the best museum men of the subsequent decades, among them Harry Francis, later director of the Cleveland Museum; A. Everett Austin, of the Hartford Atheneum and of the Ringling Museum; Henry-Russell Hitchcock, historian of architecture and curator of the museum at Smith; Alfred Barr, Philip Johnson, and Jere Abbott, who together founded the Museum of Modern Art of New York. There were also Julien Levy and Kirk Askew, who became well-known picture dealers, and Lincoln Kirstein, who almost by himself created the American ballet. There were indeed courses in painting given by the department, but only as an adjunct, principally intended to acquaint the future curators with the feel of the painter's materials and a working knowledge of the various painting techniques. This adjunct was the province of Professor Arthur Pope and Mr. Martin Mower, Professor Pope being more concerned with the theoretical aspects and Mr. Mower with the practical side of the field. In particular, Mr. Mower was in charge of a beginner's course in drawing and painting. The pleasure I was deriving from my life classes decided me to sit in on it.

Mr. Mower I remember with the greatest affection—a spry and birdlike gentleman in his early forties, dressed usually in rust-colored tweeds, his sandy moustache and reddish hair beginning to gray. He was a widower with a beautiful daughter of eleven or twelve and was full of stories of Italy, where he had studied and for which he marked his attachment by the use of little swear words like *accidenti,* Italy being then for Boston and Cambridge the same sort of promised land that Paris was for the rest of America. He was a charming painter and a kind man who encouraged my efforts and looked horribly concerned when, in my last year at Harvard, I confided to him that I had decided to become a painter.

The course was held in the barnlike attic of Sever Hall. Under Mr. Mower's guidance, we began by copying prints and drawings (I remember that there was a Japanese print and a Dürer etching) in order to find out something about line and accent and what, in the hands of a master, they could be made to do. From that we went on to drawing from the model, usually one of the students, sometimes clothed and sometimes in the nude. The even daylight of the attic room was much more agreeable to work in than the harsh flares of the night classes, and the soft gradations of tone on the model's flesh offered a much more subtle problem of rendition than the sharp black shadows I had been used to. We drew with pencil and in a sketch book. In the Boston classes, I had been taught to make my drawing big enough to fill my paper. Here, on the other hand, we were taught to draw the model the size we saw him, the size he would take on our sketch pad when viewed from where we were sitting. Working like this, the student could compare the shapes in his drawing directly with the shapes he saw in the model and easily correct the measures and proportions, much more easily than when he arbitrarily stretched the drawing to fit the paper. Drawing a thing the size one sees it is the more natural method, produces more agreeable drawings, and in fact has been the normal practice of all fine draftsmen from

---

Pisanello and Watteau to Degas and Tchelitchew. However, it must also be remembered in connection with the small size of most old master drawings that paper in their time was a scarce and valuable commodity, not to be wasted.

Here we were also taught to work in watercolor. I vividly remember buying my first painting materials at the Harvard Coop—a block of cold-pressed Watman paper, a round sable brush that came to a point (it seemed very expensive), a beautiful shiny black tin box which held brushes and paints and opened out to form a palette, and the paints themselves with their lovely names, aureolin and sienna and ultramarine, sturdy little tubes bearing the impressive label Winsor & Newton. Our first exercise in watercolor was to draw on the paper block a row of squares and fill them in with even washes of gray to make a succession of tones going down in nine regular steps from white to black. These were called the "color values" or simply the "values." The next and more difficult exercise was to execute the same value series in the various colors, in washes of viridian green, alizarin, crimson, and so on, thinned with water for the lighter squares and pulled down with black for the very darkest ones, all the while trying to keep the washes even. Once we had got some familiarity with handling tones and washes, we were set to making a pencil outline of some subject on our watercolor block—I think it was a standard still life with a plate and bottle on a table—and then filling in the spaces with washes of appropriate color and value, trying at the same time to keep the washes clean—difficult because watercolor, unlike oil, is essentially a virtuoso's medium. In oil, one mixes up a tone and puts it on—that is all there is to it. Blending is no trouble because the paint stays wet, and matching colors is no trouble; oil paint, even in drying, changes very little in tone. But watercolor washes are difficult to control. Modeling must be got by manipulating the wash before it dries, by darkening it in places with a loaded brush and picking it up in others with a dry one—a tricky affair. And if a wash is not right the first time, corrections take away its freshness and render it muddy.

Despite these difficulties, all beginners at that time invariably started off in watercolor, partly because it is particularly adapted to the sort of open-air impressionist landscape subject which then seemed the normal theme for painting, and partly because watercolor is cheaper and cleaner than oil. A set of the little tubes lasts through many a sketch, far longer than a set of oils. White, which is extravagantly used in oils, is not needed here; this is a great economy, and the messes one makes can always be cleaned off hands and clothes with a little water. The equipment is light and portable, and there is no vulnerable wet canvas to be protected on the way back home. Watercolor is practiced seated; no easel is used; the block rests on the knees. All that is needed is a small box of colors, a cup of water, a single brush, and a block of paper. The painter sets off for a walk in the country and returns with a finished picture. It is an art something like a sport and on a beach can usually be combined with sunbathing.

Sport or not, since its beginnings no one knows how long ago, the principal use of watercolor has been for sketching landscapes. Oil painting, until the tin tube was invented sometime in the early nineteenth century, had always been too cumbersome to practice outside the studio. But watercolor kits from the beginning have been easy to carry about. Little pans of pigments ground with gum have been in use since the remotest antiquity. The watercolor landscapes done from nature by the German and Flemish painters (Fig. 6) of the sixteenth century differ hardly at all from the watercolor landscapes of the early nineteenth (Fig. 7). They are all of them essentially nothing but colored drawings—careful outlines filled in with washes of color. And the smooth paper on which they are done gives them all a family resemblance.

Turner, in the early nineteenth century, brought the technique of water-color on smooth paper to its highest point. He used it for everything—sometimes as color notes for his oil landscapes; sometimes for rapidly jotting down ideas, as in the tiny sketches made at the country house of Petworth (Fig. 8), done most likely as entertainment for his host, the Earl of Egremont, and his fellow guests; sometimes for the execution of finished works, like the sets of detailed watercolor views he did on order, with their atmospheric, semiopaque washes—"scumbles" they are called—of chinese white and cobalt blue. His skill is astonishing. Nothing is more difficult to manage than a watercolor wash on smooth "hot-pressed" paper. The pigment flows to the edge of the wet patch and collects there in a hard line. Or the wash dries before the space gets filled. Wetting the paper beforehand helps, but creates other problems. Worst of all, the subsequent washes tend to dissolve and pick up the paint already put down. Additions and elaborations can indeed be made; many of Turner's best effects are got by putting one wash over another. But on smooth paper, a radical change of plan is almost impossible to conceal.

Somewhere in the middle of the nineteenth century a new kind of water-color paper appeared which made all of this easier. It was called "cold-pressed," a thick, tough, rough, rag paper, as heavy and stiff as cardboard, a paper whose rough grain would stand up under the sort of erasing and reworking which would be ruinous to a smoother surface. This heavy paper, once it had been wet, stayed damp for a long time. Washes could be flowed into one another, edges could

Fig. 6. ALBRECHT DÜRER, The Village of Kalchreuth. Watercolor. *Kunsthalle, Bremen, Germany* .

Fig. 7. THOMAS SHOTTER BOYS, Paris: the Pavillon de Flore, 1829. Watercolor. *Courtesy, Victoria & Albert Museum, London.*

Fig. 8. TURNER, An Artist at his Easel, circa 1830. Watercolor.
Courtesy The British Museum.

be blended, and highlights lifted out with a dry brush or sponge. If the paper was then allowed to dry, it could then be worked over with dry washes to get sharp details and accents. A wet technique such as this permitted all sorts of misted and muted effects impossible on hot-pressed paper even to the skill of a Turner. Throughout the rest of the century this wet technique on heavy paper was practiced with great success, particularly in England. Winslow Homer encountered it there in the eighties—as one can see from his English watercolors —and it was probably he who brought it to America.

Here in America, in our drier climate, the technique works less well; the paper dries out too quickly. Homer here, and Sargent after him in Italy, developed a technique which was still in fashion when I was introduced to the medium—heavy washes of color on rough paper, the paper now being worked on without having previously been wet. The tooth of the paper prevented anything but the most summary preliminary pencil drawing, but it held the pigment and permitted considerable reworking. One could easily glaze one wash over another if one worked fast. And on the rougher surface, the hard line of color which dried along the edges of a wash was less apparent. The pigments were put on transparently; the white of the paper shining through gave them luminosity. No body color, no chinese white mixed with the pigments, was used. Body color deadens the tone's vivacity and causes everything to turn grayer and to dry paler. One worked from light to dark, putting on the palest washes first and the darkest tones last, the whites of the picture being only the clean white paper itself left uncovered. Textures could be varied by painting with an almost dry brush. Mistakes could be corrected and highlights added by using a knife to scrape through the washes to the paper beneath. A good cold-pressed paper would even take a wash after this. And in a pinch, one could put down a blob of chinese white, and when it was dry, paint over it. But even this minimal use of body color was considered by the purists as not quite proper.

This difficult and elaborate technique was made possible by a simplified method of drawing derived from Impressionism. The pre-Impressionist drawing method had been essentially sculptural. One tried to envisage the object as a solid form, and then used the lights and shadows on it quite arbitrarily as a means of presenting this form in the round. The drawing method of the Impressionists, on the other hand, was derived from photography. The basic idea was this: If a painter could get down on his canvas the exact shapes which an object presented to his eye and give to these shapes their proper values and colors, then another eye, viewing the canvas, would receive the same sensations that the painter had received and out of them would automatically re-create the image of the object as the painter had seen it. Thus, in painting, one did not have to be aware of distance, or solidity, or space, or duration. One did not even have to know what it was that one was painting. It was sufficient to analyze what one saw into variously colored shapes of light and dark, and put them accurately each in its proper place. I will not stop here to point out how many elements of our seeing that this theory disregards. But, incomplete as it is, the method of drawing it defines made possible the virtuoso watercolor technique of Sargent and his many followers.

Looking at the Sargent watercolors today it is difficult to understand why one found them so impressive. Perhaps the colors which seemed so bright and clear have faded. Certainly, the subject matter now seems very thin—the picturesque "bits," the effects of sunlight on water and architecture that a cultivated English or American visitor would have encountered in Italy on a morning stroll. But to us at that time, their dash and evident skill were a challenge and a temptation. I spent the summer of my junior year on the beaches of Cape Cod, getting a tan and practicing the style. I believe I became fairly good at it, for on my return in the fall, Mr. Mower gave a show on the walls of our classroom in Sever Hall of the watercolors I had brought back. They could not have been very interesting. I do not remember what any of them looked like, and I have scarcely touched watercolor since.

The reason was, of course, that I had become interested in oils, and no one can do both. The techniques are as different as those of the piano and the organ. In watercolor, one works in transparent washes on a white ground. Pale tones are got with thin washes, dark tones with thick ones, and the whites of the picture are simply the white of the paper left uncovered. Thus, watercolors tend to come out pale and watery, and it is only after considerable practice that one learns to turn out pictures with strong colors and heavy values.

With oil paints it is just the opposite. One works with opaque colors on a tinted ground. And here the dark tones come out better when painted thinly, while the light tones must be laid on thick enough to hide the tone of the canvas. Since white oil paint does not have a great deal of covering power, oil paintings by beginners tend to come out dark and heavy, and considerable experience is needed before one can learn to paint in light, clear colors. The two approaches are quite incompatible and few artists have managed to use them both equally well. The lovely watercolor landscapes of Edward Lear, better known for his limericks, are incomparably finer than his oils. Cézanne's watercolors are in reality try-outs of ideas later to be done in oil. Turner, Sargent, and Winslow Homer indeed seem equally at home in both mediums, but I can think of no others.

Watercolor, as I had learned it, was a capricious medium with quite limited possibilities. Using it on smooth paper, one could range from the style of an architectural rendering to that of the tinted pencil sketches of Cézanne; or, if one were particularly skillful at it, to something approaching the more Romantic landscapes of Ruskin or Turner. Rough paper, used wet, led to Rackham and to the misty watercolors of the late nineteenth-century English school. Using it dry led straight to Homer and Sargent. Above all, watercolor was a technique adapted only to landscape painting and useless for doing any of the things that really interested me, like the solid forms of bodies and faces and the trunks of trees. Oil, as I could see from the pictures in museums, had infinitely greater possibilities. But the only practicable tradition of oil painting available to me was one which, like watercolor, derived from Impressionism.

Impressionism itself had been developed as a way of painting out-of-doors, of improvising in front of nature, and of avoiding out-moded Romantic literary associations by painting only what was present to the eye. It had come about as a reaction to the Salon picture, that laboriously detailed, studio-lit picture with sentimental subject, which had become the official expression of French Republican taste. The things which Impressionism could do, it did extremely well. But these things were few. It was virtually limited to canvases of portable dimensions executed directly from the subject. Impressionism had arrived in Boston early—the Monets of the Boston Museum are some of the finest in the world— and was still in the twenties the most advanced technique one could learn in the art schools here. In France, Impressionism had already been superseded by the School of Paris, whose right wing was formed by the followers of Cézanne, and whose left wing was Picasso and the modernist revolt. The modern movement, I and my friends at Harvard of course knew all about. We had had its principles explained and clarified by the poets S. Foster Damon and John Brooks Wheelwright, and news of its latest developments brought to us fresh from Paris by the composer Virgil Thomson, who had just returned from his first visit there. We took Dada very seriously, listened to Satie and Stravinsky, laughed over Gertrude Stein's *Tender Buttons,* and hung the walls of our studies with reproductions of Picassos and Klees. But none of this, not even Cézanne, had entered into art instruction here. The courses in painting which the

Harvard Art Department offered still derived from Impressionist theory as it had been formulated by Dr. Denman Ross, a brilliant painter and a brilliant theorist. By the time I was there, Dr. Ross no longer taught in the department. He was occasionally seen around, however, and his pictures hung on permanent show in the old Fogg Museum, in the semicircular corridor behind the auditorium. I wonder what has happened to them; I hope they have been preserved, for I remember them with great pleasure (Fig. 9).

The basis of the Impressionist technique is a system of painting in what is known as "broken color." The aim of the Impressionists had been to paint light itself, to reproduce on the canvas something equivalent to the mixtures of light which the eye receives from nature. With this in mind, they refused to mix up their tones on the palette, as everybody else had always done before them. Instead, they composed their tones on the canvas itself with tiny strokes of pure color, each stroke as vivid as possible, a confetti of different colored dots which, laid side by side and seen at a certain distance, were intended to blur in the spectator's eye to form the muted tones the painter wished to produce. All the strokes composing a tone had to match exactly in value. If any of them were darker or lighter than the others they would not blend, and the eye, instead of seeing an even tone, would see a speckling. The technique is very laborious. The tones of paint for each set of strokes must be mixed up separately, matched exactly, and kept pure. The technique lends itself readily enough to the painting of atmosphere and misty effects—that is what it was designed to do—but it becomes very difficult indeed if one wishes to paint fine details or to present solidly modeled objects. This may be one of the many things Cézanne had in mind when he said that he wished to make of Impressionism something solid like the art of the museums. And it was the difficulties of the technique which obliged Seurat—who carried broken-color as far as it would go, and did it in the studio, away from nature, guided only by color notes and theory—to stylize his drawing, to pare down the volume of his forms to the thinness of a cut-out theatre flat, and to execute his detail as a sort of embroidery on top of these flat surfaces.

Dr. Ross proposed to make the Impressionist technique easier by mixing up in advance the colors for painting his dots. For this, one took three pigments, say a yellow, a red, and a blue, and by mixing each of the pigments with varying amounts of white or black, one made up three separate series of tones, one for each pigment, descending in regular steps from a tinted white to an almost black.

Fig. 9. DENMAN ROSS, Porto Fino, circa 1930s. Watercolor.
The Fogg Art Museum, Bequest of Denman W. Ross.

26

Most important, all three colors, the yellow, the red, and the blue, of each of the seven steps must be exactly the same shade of darkness, or as it was called in the accepted terminology, have the same value. The tones were then laid out on the palette in three parallel rows with pure white paint added at the top and black at the bottom. This was called a "tempered palette" and was supposed to correspond to the tempered musical scale of the piano keyboard. It was to be "played" with as little mixing as possible. Thus, by having the pigments already laid out in tones of equal value, painting in broken-color would become relatively easy. To enrich this limited array of colors, one could add other rows of premixed pigments. One could even make up the series of tones in advance and put them up in tubes, ready to be squeezed out when needed (Col. Fig. 1).

All this sounds simple and fairly useful. Led on, however, by the analogy of the keyboard, Dr. Ross had devised another sort of tempered palette which was not simple at all. This one was based on the way that our bright colors seem to fall naturally into a regular sequence of value steps.

Let us take the brightest hues that can be got with the painter's pigments and arrange them in order going from light to dark. At the top comes the lightest, bright yellow, all by itself. At the bottom, also by itself, comes violet, the darkest of the bright colors, which is got by mixing a blue and a crimson pigment. The other bright colors come in pairs at regular intervals between the two extremes and make up a pattern of this order: at the top, bright yellow; then orange-yellow and yellow-green, both darker in tone than pure yellow; the next darkest colors are the bright orange and the bright green pair; then vermillion and blue-green; then scarlet and blue; then mauve and blue-violet; finally, alone at the bottom, violet, which is the darkest of all. Thus, as one can see there are two ways of going from light to dark, from yellow to violet, and always keeping to the brightest colors. One path leads through the greens and blues; the other through the oranges and reds (Col. Fig. 2).

In Dr. Ross's second system there were two different tempered palettes corresponding to the two different sides of the sequence, a red-orange one and a blue-green one (Col. Fig. 3). To lay out the blue-green palette, say, one would mix up the bright colors of this side of the series and lay them out in a row, putting white paint at the top and black paint at the bottom. Across from each of the colors, one placed the complement of that color, that is to say the tone one would have to mix with it to get a neutral gray. This complement has been lightened with white or brought down with black to the exact value level of its companion color. Thus, across from yellow would be a pale lavender; across from the yellow-green, a light mauve; green itself would take rose-pink; blue-green, a red; the blue, a burnt orange; blue-violet, an orange darkened with brown; and violet, a dark brown. As one can see, the first row contains the bright colors, whereas, except in the case of the vermillion-turquoise pair, the companion row of complements is composed of degraded hues and muted tones.

In the simpler palette designed for broken-color, the tones were intended to be used as they were, to be put down without further mixing in spots of bright color juxtaposed on the canvas. In the color-sequence palettes, to the contrary, mixing was permitted, but only between adjacent tones: up or down the rows to get an intermediate value, or straight across from one row to the other to dull down a tone or to get a gray. The green-blue palette I have described was for painting pictures with blues and greens at their highest intensities. The palette with the other side of the sequence was for pictures with bright reds and oranges.

As a way of going about the business of painting pictures, all this is quite as uselessly elaborate and impractical as it sounds. The palettes designed for painting broken-color were a great deal simpler and might very likely be of some use in showing a beginner how to systematize the handling of his paints. But the color-sequence palette was a completely artificial construction built on two mistaken ideas: first, on a verbal analogy between painting and music— between the painter's palette and the musical scale—which has no basis in fact; and secondly, on a notion about the nature of color now known to be inaccurate. At any rate, the color-sequence palette produced for all of us who used it the same dark and heavy color scheme with ugly purple shadows. An experienced painter might derive some entertainment from it—that is why I have put it here —as an ingenious arbitrary device which could be fun to play with. But we were by no means experienced, and it did us no good at all.

Just the same, the palettes were a fascinating toy. Mixing paints to the exact shade required and bottling them in tubes was an engrossing occupation, the most satisfactory form of mud-pie bakery. Dr. Ross himself employed his tempered palettes with ease and flexibility to produce fresh, charming color and wonderfully luminous flesh tones, though I sometimes suspect that he did not use the palettes as systematically as he pretended, and that the color charts attached to the pictures on exhibit at the Fogg were in the nature of footnotes or lists of references, post-factum addenda to endow a perhaps too graceful work with some scholastic gravity. For me and for the others in the class, however, the system was too rigid. Even the much simpler broken-color palettes seemed to render oil painting tedious and laborious. I had had no such difficulty with watercolors, where Dr. Ross's palettes could not be made to serve. And it was not until many years later, when I had scrapped it all and forgotten about it and had given up both broken-color and Impressionism, that I began to acquire some ease in handling paint.

· 3 ·

TEMPERA · FRESCO

STAINED GLASS

BYZANTINE COMPOSITION

IN MY JUNIOR year at Harvard, I took a course given by Edward Forbes, grandson of Emerson and professor of fine arts, on the materials and methods of the early Italian painters. It was held partly in the Fogg Museum and partly in the attic of the big Forbes house off Mount Auburn Street. A. Everett Austin, later director of the Hartford Atheneum and producer of Virgil Thomson's *Four Saints in Three Acts* was in the class with me. Dan Thompson, brother of the composer Randall Thompson, was Forbes's assistant. Thompson has just returned from Italy, where he had been studying fresco and tempera painting with Lokhoff (Fig. 10), who had painted the admirable copy of Benozzo Gozzoli's *The Journey of the Magi,* which decorated the stage of the Fogg auditorium, and also with Ione, who was admiringly reputed to be the author of many forgeries of Florentine pictures still hanging in museums undetected. Thompson had brought back with him an angel which he had painted in fresco and which

Fig. 10. N. LOKHOFF, copy after "The Journey of the Magi" by "Gozzoli."
Portion of a fresco in the Palazzo Medici Riccardi.
The Fogg Art Museum. Gift of Mrs. Edward M. Cary.

Mr. Sachs had complimented by mistaking it for a Botticelli. In fact, Dan Thompson was more at ease with the mechanics of the Italian painting methods than even Professor Forbes.

The text book we used was Cennino Cennini's fifteenth-century treatise on the art of painting, the only complete and practical manual of painting technique I believe in existence. Its information was, naturally enough, limited to the painting methods of Cennini's own time, but here it was complete. It was delightful reading—how to draw in charcoal and in chalk, how to make pens and ink, how to prepare a gesso panel and how to gild it, how to grind the pigments and how to temper them with egg so that they could be used to paint with, how to color faces and what colors to use for various kinds of drapery, how to prepare a wall for fresco, how to paint on it and how, using egg, to retouch it after it was dry, how the yolk of a city-laid egg is paler than a country one, how students should refrain from lifting heavy weights, which would make the hand tremble, and so on—all told in the straightforward manner of an assured and unpretentious workman.

The course began with a gesso panel, the traditional support for tempera painting, which we prepared according to Cennini's precise directions. For this, one took a panel of well-seasoned wood or heavy plyboard, gave it a couple of coats of thin glue size to seal the pores, and then on top of this, six or seven thin coats of gesso (a mixture of glue size and powdered chalk or whiting kept warm and liquid in a double boiler), each coat being given time to cool and set before the next was applied. When the layer of gesso was thick enough—an eighth of an inch or so—it was sandpapered to an ivory-smooth surface and got ready for gilding by painting it with thin washes of armenian bole, a very fine-textured, soft, red clay, powdered and mixed with a little glue and water. One wash after another was put on till the white was covered with an even red. This coat of bole and glue, when dampened, served to attach the gold—real gold leaf, which was laid on in sheets and then burnished with a hook-shaped piece of onyx till it became as dark and shining as polished metal.

In the early tempera pictures, the background to the figures was generally in gold; the whole panel was gilded except the parts which were to be painted in tempera. A raised and ornamental border, built as part of the panel and gilded along with it, served as frame, and it is quite likely that the fashion which we still have for gold frames on oil paintings comes down to us directly from these carved and gilded edgings.

A "tempera" is something which will temper a pigment, in other words, turn it into paint. And the tempera used by Cennini to bind the pigments to the gesso was the simple yellow of an egg, with nothing added but a little water and a drop of vinegar to keep the egg from going bad too quickly. This was only for the painter's comfort; rotten egg apparently binds just as well as fresh. To prepare tempera, one puts dry pigment on the grinding slab, adds enough plain water to make a watery mud, and, using a muller, grinds the mixture smooth. A little of the mud is put in a cup, mixed in some egg yellow, and thinned with water for painting. A series of cups are needed, a separate cup for each shade of color to be used in painting, and the whole series must be kept around until the picture has been finished. This is quite indispensable; all the tones dry lighter and in a very irregular way, and once a tone is dry, it is almost impossible to match it with a fresh mixture of egg and pigments. The vinegar used as preservative is not very effective, nor is the oil of cloves or the benzoate of soda which are sometimes used instead. And a tempera painter's studio, and his recently painted pictures as well, generally smell strongly of the hen coop.

One starts a tempera picture by laying in the outlines with pen and brown ink, and then goes on to tempera, using small round sable brushes. The modeling of the hands and faces is begun with three tones of green—a light, a middle, and a dark—made from *terra verde*, a greenish earth, mixed with white lead. On top of this green foundation, the modeling is done all over again in pink—white lead and a red earth color mixed to the same three shades. The modeling is executed in a loose cross-hatching, like the network of lines used for shading in steel engravings, and the interplay of pink with the green, which still shows through, serves to give the orange-tan tone of flesh. The colors to be used for painting clothes and drapery are equally conventionalized. The folds and modeling are painted first in one color and then repainted in another, and Cennini furnishes explicit directions as to which pigment to use for each kind and color of cloth.

Once the egg is thoroughly dry, it is quite insoluble. Actually, egg tempera is much more durable than oil, tougher and less subject to decay. Tempera also keeps its color better than oil, for, unlike oil, it does not darken or yellow, and pigments ground in it, particularly the blues, remain incomparably brighter. It protects the surface it is painted on, as oil does not, for it does not turn acid to corrode the wood or canvas as oil tends to do. It requires no varnish to protect it, and a slight rubbing with a soft cloth produces all the sheen that one wants.

With all these advantages, tempera nevertheless remains a medium for draftsmen, useful only in techniques based on line. The broader sorts of painting such as have been practiced since the Renaissance, the techniques based on patterns of lights and darks and on areas and masses, are not possible with it; smooth transitions from one tone to another are too difficult to execute. Here, no blending of the wet paint is possible; the tempera dries too fast. Besides, the paint piles up at the edges of the brushstroke to dry there in a darker ridge, so that each stroke remains visible as an individual line and gradations of tone must be got with tiny cross-hatchings, small brushes, and considerable labor. Large areas with even gradations, such as one needs for the play of light and shadow on a wall or in a niche behind a figure become particularly troublesome.

These difficulties were somehow resolved by the later tempera painters, who seem to have had much less trouble with their gradations and their brushstrokes. How they did it, nobody knows exactly, for there are no painting manuals extant from this later time. Perhaps by skill of hand alone, though this seems doubtful. More likely it was accomplished with some particular admixture of varnish or cooked oil or something else (there are even obscure references in contemporary books to the use of fig milk) which rendered the paint more malleable and unctuous; or even perhaps the use of some particular sort of brush —a spatula with a leather tip has been suggested. At any rate, the paintings of later tempera painters like Filippino Lippi do not show the outlined brushstroke, and their gradations of tone in modeling have a smooth fluidity impossible with Cennini's unsophisticated egg yolk.

But even with these problems solved, it still remains that tempera changes tone enormously in drying and that matching a fresh, wet color with one already dry is a matter of pure guesswork. The painter Tom Prentiss, who knows egg tempera well, tells me that if dry tempera paint is washed over with water, it returns temporarily to the tone it had when wet and can then easily be matched with fresh color. This may well work; I have not tried it. But even then, the principal objection to egg tempera for contemporary use has not been met: egg tempera will not lend itself to the sort of improvisation which is the basis of the painting of our time. A picture in tempera must be planned in advance. Every detail must be established from the beginning. The composition cannot be changed during the progress of the work, as we today are accustomed to do. So that tempera remains a draftsman's medium, excellent when using a prearranged set of colors to paint from drawings, as the early Italians did, but almost impossible to use in painting freely from nature.

Just the same, as an antiquarian reconstruction, egg tempera was fascinating to work with, and for my class exercise I copied the drapery of a figure in a small picture (Fig. 11) by the North Italian painter Cosimo Tura. I am afraid, nevertheless, that I learned less about the technique of tempera painting than about the intricacies of drapery which characterize the Gothic style. But even this small experience with tempera was later to be useful when I discovered that one of the tempera emulsions provided a very easy way and, as it turned out later, a very risky one, of beginning an oil painting.

Fresco, which we went on to next, has not proved useful, though it then seemed very promising on account of the success Diego Rivera was having with it in Mexico. To paint in fresco, one needs only dry earth colors in powder, well-slaked lime for the white, and a dry and solid wall to paint on. We used for wall the attic rooms of the big Forbes house, and for lime, some which had been slaking for a year or more in the back yard under Dan Thompson's supervision. The fresco process is laborious. It begins with a cartoon—a detailed drawing on heavy paper of the exact size the fresco is to be. The wall itself is made ready with a preparatory coat, put down with a certain amount of grain and left to dry. The cartoon is put up on the wall and the outlines of the drawing are traced through onto the rough plaster. The painting is then begun by covering a portion of the tracing, as much as the painter thinks he can finish in one day, with a coat of smooth wet plaster. On this fresh plaster, he restores the outlines which have been covered up by putting the cartoon back in place and retracing it on to the soft plaster with the end of a brush. This indented outline remains visible in the finished fresco, so that on the walls of the Sistine Chapel, for example, one can see where Michelangelo followed his original drawings and where he thought he changed them.

Large cartoons on paper, however, are a late-fifteenth-century device. The early fresco painters did not use them. Paper was expensive and came in small sheets. As one can see from the frescos removed from Florentine buildings injured by the Arno River floods of several years ago, the early fresco painters worked out their compositions by drawing in red chalk directly on the rough preparatory plaster coating of the wall.

The paint for fresco is nothing but powdered pigment mixed with water. Slaked lime serves for white. One works as in tempera with drawing strokes and cross-hatchings, making flesh tones, as in tempera, with pink painted over green. The plaster will accept the pigments and incorporate them into its surface as long as it remains wet. One has four or five hours, depending on the dampness of the wall itself and on the season of the year. Once the plaster begins to dry, the pigment and water mixture will no longer take on it. At this point, one chips

Fig. 11. COSIMO TURA (circa 1430–1495), Adoration of the Magi. Tempera on panel. *Fogg Art Museum. Gift of Mrs. Edward M. Cary.*

off from the wall whatever one has not been able to finish that day, undercutting the edges of the plaster so that the next day's section can be joined to it smoothly. These joints remain visible in the finished fresco, and one can tell by counting the sections of any fifteenth-century fresco how many days the painter took to finish the job.

The Roman frescos of Herculaneum and Pompeii could never have been executed by anything like Cennini's process, simply because their plaster has no joints. Since their surface also shows a sort of waxy polish, it is supposed that they were done in some form of encaustic, a painting method based on wax, which did not need to be painted on wet plaster and so did not have to be finished piecemeal as Cennini's frescos did.

Just as in tempera, the tones to be used in a fresco are mixed in advance and preserved in a series of jars. Fresco dries lighter and paler, a great deal paler even than tempera does, and tones, once dry, are difficult to match with wet pigments. The pigments used are principally the earth colors—the ochers, siennas, umbers, and green earths—which furnish a whole range of degraded hues, from green and brown and yellow through orange and red to purple. Blue in fresco painting has always been a problem. Real ultramarine, the only safe bright blue the Italians had, tends to react chemically with the lime in the plaster and must be painted on later and in tempera. The same must be done with the bright red pigments, vermillion and madder, so that red draperies were usually underpainted in a duller red-earth pigment, as were also the skies. This accounts for the red skies found in some of the Italian frescos where the blue, put on in tempera, has scaled off and disappeared. True fresco itself, however, is very solid. The lime, in setting, absorbs carbon dioxide from the air to become a form of marble, making a very permanent surface, provided that the wall is not humid and the climate is a dry one and there is no coal smoke in the air. Today, with the canopy of smoke which hangs over our cities and comes down in the rain as sulphurous acid, the fresco process cannot be considered permanent.

Cennini's fresco was as far into the Italian methods as the course took us. The Venetians we scarcely touched on, probably because there does not exist any authoritative treatise comparable to Cennini's which could explain how these Venetians painted. The method is generally supposed to have begun with an underpainting executed in monochrome, the color being applied later in the form of transparent glazes. Under Mr. Mower's direction, we had made some vague attempt at this, executing the underpainting for a picture in a monochrome of bright blue-green—viridian, it was—and glazing the local colors on top of this

38

with transparent browns and blues and scarlets. The results were garish and glossy and had none of the warmth and subtlety of the Venetian masters. Besides this, we did our underpaintings in oil, which took a long time to dry, especially when it had been put on thick enough to hide the grain of the canvas. And unless the underpainting is thoroughly dry before it is glazed, there is always danger of the picture cracking. To play safe, one had to wait weeks before going on with the rest of the work. Also, the transparent glazes we used tended to settle in the interstices of brushstroke and canvas grain in a most unpleasant and unmanageable way.

To judge from the results, our method could have had little in common with the methods of the Venetians. To begin with, the paint used by them for glazing could not have been as systematically transparent as we supposed. It must have had a certain opacity and body, and the vehicle it was put on with must have been more complicated than oil alone. Moreover, the Venetian underpaintings could not have been done, as ours were, in oil-ground pigments. The slow drying of the oil paint would have entailed a very inconvenient delay before the next step of the process could be undertaken. One is forced to imagine some mysterious painting medium, possibly an emulsion, composed of oil, glue, egg, wax, varnish, and God knows what else, which would harden rapidly enough to be worked on top of without too much waiting, and at the same time, would blend smoothly like oil, and, like oil, would not change tone too much in drying.

The great series of Tintorettos in the Scuola di S. Rocco in Venice (Fig. 12), at any rate, was probably not executed in any of the oil or varnish paints we know about. Their present state would indicate a quite different medium. The pictures today are unnaturally dark. What should be bright colors are now tones of brown and dirty gray. Besides this, the color-values are inconsistent—dark passages which contain details far too light for the context, and outlines which are too dark and sometimes even double, as if the upper layers of paint had become transparent and the sketchy beginning layout of the composition were showing through.

This is certainly not the way that Tintoretto left them. In fact, when the pictures were taken down for safekeeping during the First World War, it was found that the edge of one of them had been turned under the frame, and thus protected, and had preserved its original color. This edge, a six-inch border of green leaves and red fruit, is still today brighter than Renoir. The air of Venice is not corrosive enough, even now, to account for such a change. Other Tintorettos, those in the Academia, for example, have not darkened like this, nor can the

Fig. 12. TINTORETTO, Apparition of S. Rocco. Oil on canvas. Scuola di S. Rocco, Venice. *Photograph courtesy of Alinari–Anderson.*

deterioration of the S. Rocco series be blamed on a vice in the paint itself. Otherwise the same changes would have taken place in the protected strip. It seems more reasonable to believe that the S. Rocco pictures had been painted in some sort of glue-sized medium of the kind that is used today for painting stage sets and theatre backdrops—water-thinned, easy and rapid to apply, and drying to a flat and porous surface. The rapidity with which Tintoretto is known to have executed his work makes this seem all the more possible. If this is so, then their present state can easily be accounted for by supposing that, sometime in the nineteenth century, an ill-advised restorer treated them to a coat of heavy oil varnish which penetrated into the porous paint surface, rendered the upper layers transparent, disclosed details which had been painted out, and falsified the color values, and that it is this varnish, now darkened with age to a dirty brown, which has reduced the pictures to the blackened monochromes one sees today.

At any rate, the problem of how the Venetians painted, exactly what they used and how they went about it, has puzzled painters ever since, has never been satisfactorily solved, and has produced all sorts of improbable methods and impermanent results. I have done my share in this experimentation and will speak of my trials and failures when I get to them.

This was my last year at Harvard. I had to find a job, and all I knew was mathematics. A mathematical major today is a prize to be fought over by physics laboratories and state departments. In my time, a degree in mathematics led only to teaching it, which I did not wish to do. Fortunately, a classmate presented me to Charles Connick, who ran a shop in Boston making stained-glass windows. Connick inspected a sample of my work, a drawing of a head in profile, and took me on at once.

Connick was the best known stained-glass maker in America, a specialist in the Gothic-revival style which was the most popular style for American ecclesiastical architecture. Only Christian Science held apart. This religion, a newcomer with New England origins, patronized the Georgian style and, at a respectful distance, followed Wren. Elsewhere, the official dress of Protestantism was the Gothic. The Methodists and Baptists were, in general, content with a rounded and somewhat dumpy form of the idiom, while the Presbyterians and Episcopalians, particularly the more prosperous communities, preferred to follow the vertical and aspiring model of Chartres or Ely. Ralph Adams Cram was the foremost American architect in this form of the Gothic, and most of Connick's work was done for him and in the French thirteenth-century manner, which Cram favored. The library of Connick's shop was well supplied with color plates of Viollet-le-Duc's reconstructions of the windows of the Sainte Chapelle and Notre Dame of Paris, and with splendid photographs of the windows of all the great Gothic churches—Poitiers, Le Mans, and the others (Fig. 13)—with their thick and heavy drawing lines and shockingly vigorous faces. I must confess that in Connick's own windows a great deal of the pre-Raphaelite softness always seemed to intrude, and I suspect that the churchmen who were his clients had somewhat more sympathy for Burne-Jones than for the Romanesque.

The shop occupied a loft in downtown Boston. A great deal of it was given over to vertical bins holding an enormous stock of glass sheets in fragments of all sizes and colors. Connick himself, who had a wonderful way with bishops, originated the ideas and designs. Tracing the shapes of the windows from the architect's blueprints, he would make small watercolor sketches with color and figures roughly indicated, explicit enough, however, to give the architect and his clients a clear idea of how the finished window would look, and detailed enough for us, the secondary designers and glass cutters, to follow.

I was one of three secondary designers. Our job was to enlarge Connick's original sketch into a black-and-white cartoon the actual size the window was to be, a cartoon which served as guide for cutting and for painting the innumerable pieces of colored glass of which such a window is composed. We worked in charcoal, drawing in the figures with their faces, hands and drapery, the architectural or diapered backgrounds and ornamental borders, using black lines rather than shading, establishing the shapes of the pieces of glass from which the window would be made, and outlining these shapes with thick, heavy lines the exact width of the lead mouldings which would eventually hold the pieces together. The cartoon finished, it was handed over to the glass cutters, who first traced out the pattern of our lead lines in black paint on a large piece of clear glass, then cut out pieces of colored glass in the shapes indicated by our cartoons and in the colors shown in Connick's watercolor sketch. The pieces were then stuck with blobs of wax, each in its proper place, onto the plate of clear glass which was then propped up against the studio window for inspection. Tones could be changed and pieces added till the color came out right. Connick's windows generally ran to a contrast of reds and blues, with just enough green and brown added to keep the combination from going too purple. If a tone was not dark enough, the glass could be doubled or even tripled. Tiffany, in the 1900s, had practiced a wonderfully costly version of such doubling for naturalistic effects. He would search through the enormous stocks of marbled glass he kept on hand until he had turned up a piece whose ripple marks would more or less imitate the feathers of a

42

Fig. 13. Head of the Prophet Jeremiah, circa 1225. Stained glass. Probably from a choir window of the Cathedral of Lyon. *Paris: Dépôt des Monuments historiques.*

wing or the folds of the piece of drapery he intended to represent, and then he would back the marbled piece with pieces of colored glass to give it the hue he needed. Tiffany had also used colored enamels, of the sort employed in china painting, which he baked into the glass to give pink flesh tones and realistic modeling to the hands and faces. Connick, following the older tradition, disdrained such up-to-date effects and limited himself to black paint for modeling. However, it was not considered a violation of the tradition to etch through the thin layer of color on "flashed" glass to get a white design on a red or blue ground (as in a Bohemian goblet), or to stain a yellow design on clear glass by painting it with a silver salt and firing it—very useful when it came to showing crowns and jewels. But on the whole, black was more respectable. This was got with an iron oxide and a flux ground together with oil or with glue to make a paint. The glue paint gave rather cleaner lines. When fired, the paint fused to become part of the glass and just as indestructible.

Once the colors of the window had been satisfactorily balanced, the glass painters took over; placing the pieces of colored glass in place on our cartoon, they traced our lines and shadings on them with the oxide paint. The pieces were then fired and the window reassembled with wax on the big glass plate for inspection. Pieces were changed if needed, and the whole was given a patina of oxide paint stippled on, which served both to soften the whiter places, which were apt to glare, and to imitate the dirt of age. The pieces were then refired, leaded together, fastened to the iron frames which had been made for them, and shipped off to their churches.

As I have said, the shop worked in what was considered the thirteenth-century tradition. That is to say that Connick's glass did not pretend to imitate oil painting. The draperies and faces were not modeled in chiaroscuro, nor was there any attempt at naturalistic background or perspective. The drawing was entirely linear, with heavy black lines to indicate the features in faces, the veinings in leaves, and the folds in drapery. This linear drapery was a Byzantine-Romanesque convention (Fig. 14), derived from the drapery in Classic Greek and Roman sculpture by way of cruder local imitations. It was a stylization practiced all over the Early Christian world, a stylization in which thighs and forearms came out as flat ovals surrounded by garlands of lines, and the falls of drapery were indicated by cascades of lines ending up in neat hooks. The lines we used were carefully shaped and tapered. They had to be thick to be visible. In painted windows such as these, a light will always spread and eat into the darks, and the

Fig. 14. Gospels, in Latin. Amiens, end of 11th century. Stained glass. *Bibliothèque Municipale.*

smallest scratch in a dark area, when seen from a distance, becomes a marked and visible hole. The lines were also what is known as "strong" ones—that is to say, they ended crisply in a snap. A "weak" curve, in this sort of linear design, is a line which starts out as if to end in a snap, and then goes on to do something else. A clear illustration of this kind of line can be found in any piece of Art Nouveau furniture, a style whose peculiar character depends entirely on a systematic use of the weak curve. Deprived of this, Art Nouveau would be only another form of Gothic Revival, differing only in its affection for flower forms like the poppy, the cattail, and the water lily which the real Gothic workmen had not thought to employ.

Another characteristic of the Byzantine-Romanesque linear-style design is the care given to the empty spaces. In this sort of composition, any liberty can be taken in drawing and perspective as long as the areas of background surrounding the objects and figures come out in interesting shapes. The Romanesque frescoes in the churches of Catalonia are an excellent example of this (Fig. 15), where the most carefully studied part of the design is the shape of the bare, unfinished plaster in which the figures are set. Picasso himself seems to have been influenced by these frescoes. At any rate, one finds the same approach to design in the massive and rather frightening seated women which he was doing in the early 1940s (Fig. 16).

In flat linear design such as this, the lines cannot be permitted to lead out of the picture. They must direct the eye toward the important elements, to focal points like hands and faces, and continually force the attention back to them. Take for example the group of figures surrounding Justinian and Theodora in the mosaics of the church of San Vitale in Ravenna. No matter where one looks, the eye is constantly brought back to the principal figures. This is contrived by the way the lines of drapery fall and follow and point. The sixteenth-century Germans practiced a similar but rather more mechanical device for composing a picture. In any engraving by Dürer (Fig. 17), for example, or for that matter, in any painting by Vermeer (Fig. 18), the basis of the composition is always a network of diagonal, horizontal, and vertical straight lines. If one takes a ruler and extends these lines until they touch the frame, one will find that the point of intersection of any two of them will lie either on the edge of the picture or on a line in the picture which is parallel to this edge. This mesh of constantly intersecting but partly interrupted lines acts to lead the eye away from the frame and trap it within the picture.

46

Fig. 15. Upholders of the Firmament. Detail of fresco
from a Spanish Catalan Romanesque chapel, Santa
Maria du Muir. *Boston Museum of Fine Arts,
Purchase of R. J. Bosch from the Evans Fund.*

Fig. 16. PICASSO, Femme en Vert, 1943. *Collection Mr. and Mrs. James Johnson Sweeney.*

Fig. 17. ALBRECHT DÜRER, Melancholia I. Engraving. *The Metropolitan Museum of Art. Harris Brisbane Dick Fund, 1943.*

Fig. 18. VERMEER, Lady with a Lute. Oil on canvas.
The Metropolitan Museum of Art. Bequest of Collis P. Huntington, 1925.

Notice how the lines lead back to the eye, the mouth, and the pearls.

All this is a quite different form of design and of drawing from the Cosimo Tura I had copied at the Fogg Museum. In the Byzantine-Romanesque tradition, which our stained glass followed, nothing is new or original. Everything is made up on well-tried formulas, as one can see in the traditional icons still being painted in Greece today, in which the faces and attitudes and groupings of the figures appearing in the various sacred subjects—Saint George and the Dragon, the Ascension of Christ, and so on—have remained unchanged for the last five hundred years. Beginning with Giotto, however, the Byzantine formulas were little by little abandoned to be replaced by direct observation of nature. In the work of Giotto and of the Italian and Flemish painters who followed him, the drapery is no longer an abstract pattern of lines. It has become a real and solid thing, painted after drawings made from real cloth worn by live models or draped over lay figures. A particularly good drawing would be kept on hand as part of a workshop's equipment, so that one occasionally finds the same piece of drapery repeated, perhaps in a different color, in another of the workshop's pictures. This solidly modeled drapery is nearer to sculpture in its conception than to flat design. What goes on within the outline is vastly more important than the more or less accidental shapes the outline cuts out of the background (Fig. 19). All this leads away from the conception of background as a flat space that must be made interesting. It introduces instead the notion of background as a volume of air contained between the horizon and the surface of the picture, a volume to be filled with trees, mountains, buildings, people, what you will. On this notion is founded the naturalistic conception of painting which has been held throughout the world well into our century, a conception in which a painting is regarded as a representation of some possible or imaginable world lying outside our eyes.

A painting in the Byzantine-Romanesque tradition, on the other hand, is a tapestry, a way of enriching a surface, and must lie flat on the plane it decorates. No one thing should be strong enough to stand out. In a stained-glass window, this means that there should be a certain unity in the color values; nothing should be white or light enough to stick out or make a hole. This was precisely one of the difficulties with Connick's windows. Here the faces and hands had to be white or, with the exception of the Three Magi, at least light enough to be appropriate to the Caucasian race. The bishops would not have liked it otherwise. The pale areas always transmitted too much light, even when they had been toned down with a heavy patina, and tended to recede into the window as much too brilliant

Fig. 19. FRA ANGELICO, St. Dominic. Fresco in San Marco, Florence.
Photograph courtesy of Alinari–Anderson.

Fig. 21. DANTE GABRIEL ROSETTI, Mrs. Wm. Morris. Red chalk on paper.
The Metropolitan Museum of Art. Gift of Jessie Lemont Trausil, 1947.

Fig. 22. AUBREY BEARDSLEY, Salome: The Climax. *The Frick Collection.*

I worked at being a stained-glass designer for some eight or ten months. In the meantime, I had been making portrait drawings in red chalk of everyone I knew at Cambridge. I gave a show of them at the Grace Horne Gallery in Boston and received from Harvard a two-year traveling fellowship to study painting abroad. It was my first and to this day my last official honor. And in the fall of 1925 I set out for Paris, equipped with a sound training in drawing, considerable practice in linear design, and no idea at all how to go about painting in oil.

· 4 ·

PARIS · NEW YORK
AND MURAL PAINTING

NOW THAT I HAD at length got to Paris to study painting, I still found it difficult to believe that I had a talent for it. Even the award of a Harvard fellowship was not enough to convince me. My gift had come to light when I was almost grown, much too late for me to accept it naturally as an integral part of my makeup or to put much trust in its guidance. People whose abilities appear in childhood, the Picassos, the Mozarts, the Menuhins, are never bothered by such doubts. As far back as they can remember, their talent has been the basic framework of their identity. Living with it has given them authority. They have known from the beginning that if they follow its dictates, everything they do will come out right. As a result, their early work, if not as original as their more mature production, will nevertheless appear professional and assured.

A latecomer like myself has none of this self-confidence, nor does he acquire it until much later in his career. He is not yet sure of his newfound abilities. His talent is all the more suspect to him because he does not yet understand the difference between talent and facility. He is shocked to learn that he has no facility whatever outside the narrow field in which his talent is willing to operate, to realize how little control he has of what it will or will not do, to discover that when he tries to make use of it to please a client, or to advance his career by forcing it to follow some current fashion, it simply disappears. In addition, if he has had a scholastic education, his critical sense will have developed far beyond his technical abilities, and he will be driven to disparage his own work. He has become acquainted with the great masters of the past, but he has not yet learned that the work of the dead and the work of the living are completely different in kind—that the dead form part of the cataloged past, while the living belong to the still-unclassified future, and that these are two incongruent orders of existence which cannot by any exercise of judgment or imagination be compared. He will nevertheless place his picture beside the masterpieces of the past and lose all courage at the confrontation. And, at the end of his working day, when he is too tired to see anything but his inadequacies, he is only too ready to yield to his discouragement and tear his picture up.

Gertrude Stein once remarked—I am always quoting this—that a young painter does not need criticism; what he needs is praise. He knows better than anybody what is wrong with his work. What he does not know is what is right with it. Its real qualities, he is even apt to find inelegant and somewhat embarrassing. For the young painter in such circumstances I have what I believe is some very useful advice. First, never go on painting after you have become tired and have stopped seeing (Cézanne said this too). Second, when the painting session is over, turn the picture to the wall and have the courage not to look at it again till you pick it up for the next session. Third is a rule by which to know whether or not the picture is going well. If you forget about it after you have quit working, everything is fine. But if you continue to think about it, either with pride or worry, something has gone wrong, and it must be left alone for a day or two, until the mind has cleared and you can see the picture fresh.

At any rate, here I was in Paris, the dream city of all art students, still unsure of my talent but willing to give it a chance and not at all certain how to go about it. All I could think of was another art school, and I enrolled in the old Académie Julian on the Rue du Dragon. It was all very much what I had left in Boston— a large atelier with students, a model, and instructors who came in to give criticism once a week. The classroom was larger and grubbier than in Boston, with skylights which had never been washed for fear that the neighbors might look in.

The instructors were more old-fashioned and conservative than in Boston, and the students, though younger, rowdier, and more entertaining, were all turning out laborious "academies" in tired charcoal. This was getting me nowhere, and after a month I left. Then I tried a school run by André Lhote, an eclectic modernist with a considerable reputation, a talented and agreeable artist whose classes were said to be the most advanced available. These were held in a smaller, cleaner room, with a model to draw from and students doing almost the same sort of academic life-class studies as at Julian's, a little fresher, perhaps, and for the most part with incongruous Cubist-style planes and directional lines added to the background to trademark the exercises as modern. Lhote himself came in three or four times a month to correct our work and give talks analyzing pictures—one, I seem to remember, was a color print of a Corot or Daubigny landscape—explaining their composition and color schemes according to abstract principles which, had I been more mature, I would have found extremely interesting and useful, but which at that time I could neither understand nor accept.

Leaving Lhote's, I went for a month to Jacovleff and then to the sculptor Bourdelle. Jacovleff was a Russian painter who had accompanied the first Citroën expedition across Africa (Fig. 23) and had acquired an international reputation with his precise and highly individual drawings of the native tribesmen done in red and black chalks. To my disappointment, for I admired his work enormously, Jacovleff himself never turned up. The school was being run by an assistant through whom, at second hand, the students were learning to imitate the tubular modeling characteristic of Jacovleff's style, which he produced by drawing with the flat side of the chalk stick. Bourdelle, on the other hand, a large, heavy man with a beard, did come to his classes but obviously did not like doing it. He showed something of a contempt for his students and teased us unmercifully.

By the time my month was out, I had decided that I did not want to become a sculptor, that I had had enough life-class drawing, and that it was time to start painting on my own. I had learned nothing from the classes, and still went about painting as if it were only a way of drawing in oils. For a while I shared a studio with William Littlefield, a painter and classmate from Harvard. We hired as a model an African dancer I had encountered at George Antheil's, and we each did a picture of him. Littlefield's I remember as brilliant and skillful, not too good as a characterization, but a much better integrated picture than mine. As for the one I did, the figure, which was completed in a few poses, came out with a rather striking presence, but the background, an invented one, I worked on for months and never managed to pull off. During that winter, I also did some still lifes, stiff

Fig. 23. ALEXANDER JACOVLEFF, African Tribesman, circa 1922. *Collection Dr. Charles Poindexter.*

and with little interest, and finally, toward the spring, I finished the only production of that year interesting enough to be remembered or regretted—a portrait of the poet Sherry Mangan in the nude, curled up in a big wing armchair as if asleep. It had nacreous flesh (from Dr. Ross's Impressionist-style tempered palettes), a circular reentering composition (from my training at Connick's in linear design), and an enormous hamlike thigh, the direct influence, though I did not then realize it, of Picasso's fat ladies of the period.

Paris was strong medicine, very different from the easy communal university life I had been used to, and more than a little upsetting. There were plenty of interesting people around, many of whom to this day remain my dearest friends, but I seemed to find no lead that would help introduce me to the traditions of painting or give me some facility in handling oils. Also, I was convinced that painting could be properly done only in a studio—an absurd idea but one which I held onto for years—and in Paris studios were impossible to find. I did however manage to rent one for the summer in Cagnes-sur-Mer. The next winter I ran away from Paris and stayed in Anticoli Corrado outside Rome, where studios were to be had and villagers could be hired to pose. There I did some drawings, a couple of landscapes, some undigested figure pieces, and in the summer returned to America. I had had almost two years in Europe. I had seen Paris, Rome, Florence, and Milan and a great many people, pictures, and monuments. And now I found myself in New York with no money and knowing very little more about painting in oil than when I left.

The pictures I had brought back with me were promising enough, but they were, like all students' work, not uniform in style, and there were too few successful ones among them to make up an exhibition. My fellowship was over, and I had to stop working at painting and get a job. So I turned to the one thing in which I had professional training and found work with a stained-glass maker on Twenty-third Street, drawing cartoons depicting a series of saints appropriate to what I was told was to be a Byzantine church in the Bronx. When the job was done, I found steadier employment as an assistant to the mural painters Victor White and Barry Faulkner.

At that time, the end years of the twenties, mural painting was having a considerable vogue. A mural in the lobby or board room of a great business corporation had something of the same status value that the big-name, big-area abstractions hold today. It was partly because murals were known to be expensive, and partly on account of the prestige then held by the mural painters Sert and Rivera. Sert was patronized principally by decorators and by the cultivated rich, who

---

found in him a revival of the decorative style of Pillement and the Rococo. Rivera was admired by the intellectuals, on account of his sophisticated primitivism based on a mixture of Aztec and Giotto, and by the liberals, on account of the Marxian content of his work. Rivera's prestige was in fact so great that, despite his Communism, he was patronized even by Ford and the Rockefellers. And here his doctrinal truculence caused considerable public scandal. His frescoes for the interior court of the Detroit Art Museum which Ford commissioned have survived the tempest. But his murals in Rockefeller Center, which insolently and gratuitously mocked his client, were removed and replaced by the politically noncommittal work of his rival Sert.

Barry Faulkner was by no means as famous as either of these two and worked in a less personal style. He nevertheless enjoyed a solid reputation and received important commissions, particularly from business firms. His jobs were usually large enough to require the aid of several assistants. Victor White had a smaller and more local (New York) reputation. His painting style was not spectacular, but he was adaptable and competent. He usually worked on smaller commissions than Faulkner's, usually for private clients, and for the most part got his jobs through decorators. During the time I was with them as an assistant, Faulkner did a large mural with stylized allegorical figures of Commerce, Electricity, and so on, and a wall-sized decorative map of a small section of the Argonne, where his client had fought in World War One. I was with Victor White somewhat longer and helped, among other things, on a cartoon of a male figure symbolizing Electricity for the mosaic half dome which was to decorate the entrance doorway of a downtown office building, and with the dining room walls of a private house in Boston which he covered with Chinese trees and children on a silver ground, suitably styled to set off a fine suite of Chinese Chippendale.

Commissions from decorators, such as this dining room, were usually undertaken and executed without any particular formality. The decorator already knew the painter's work and would know what to expect. But when the painter was dealing with committees on important official jobs, there was an elaborate routine that had to be gone through. First, the painter prepared a small watercolor sketch of the proposed mural, reduced to the scale of a quarter of an inch to the foot, in color, and with the subject—the figures, background, and so on—shown as explicitly as is possible in this small size. For presentation to the committee, the sketch was mounted in a dollhouse replica of the room where the mural was intended to go, a tiny model with all the moldings and other architectural details to scale and in their proper colors. When the small sketch had been approved by the committee, the painter enlarged it to make a working sketch from which the mural itself would be painted. This was a careful watercolor done in the much larger scale of an inch or even an inch and a half to the foot, with both the color and the drawing all worked out in detail. Following the indications of the working sketch, the painter and his assistants ran up the full-size cartoon for the work in charcoal on brown paper. The canvas was then hung on the studio wall and the cartoon traced through onto it. Again with the working sketch as guide, the colors to be used on the mural were mixed up in oil paint, the principal tones in quite large quantities, and the actual painting of the mural was at length begun. As one can see, a great deal of this work could be entrusted to assistants, who could also be expected to paint in the ground tones, the borders, and the minor details.

The mural had to be finished in the painter's studio. Little could be done to it after it was in place. Any large commission such as I have described would certainly be destined for a union-built building, where it would be cemented to the wall by members of the Painters and Paperhangers Union, and any subsequent painting on it could be done only by a member of that union, to which the painter himself could scarcely hope to belong. Thus, if there were any retouches or changes to be made, the painter was obliged to stand below and tell a union member on the scaffold what to do; though I have heard of cases where a friendly or corruptable member would keep watch at the door while the painter did his own correcting. With such a limitation, real fresco executed in wet plaster on the wall itself, was out of the question. And as for the mural in oil on canvas, once it was in place, any radical correction or changes became impossible. Hence it was most important for the painter to know before beginning the work the exact colors of the walls and stone and woodwork which would frame it. Otherwise, it could never be made to harmonize with its setting. This is probably what happened with the murals which Puvis de Chevannes executed in France for the Boston Public Library. Puvis must have been given a sample of the wrong marble, for the blue-green tonality of the paintings is perfect for pale gray freestone, but quite out of key with the cornices and pilasters of yellow marble in which they are actually set.

A mural painted under the system I have described is most unlikely to exhibit the qualities which we admire in the wall paintings of the past. The reasons for this have very little to do with the relative talents of the painters. To begin with, when a carefully finished sketch is carefully enlarged, its freshness is inevitably lost. The felicities of color, handling, and drawing which the sketch exhibits—in fact, the pleasing effects of paint in any picture at all—are the result of a series of accidents, of imperceptible minglings, thicknesses, and transparencies of paint that have happened during the course of painting, and that the painter has liked and preserved. These effects, produced by accident, cannot be copied or enlarged, even by the painter himself, no matter how hard he tries. Each spot of color in the sketch owes its vivacity to innumerable minute variations of tone. When the sketch is redone on a larger canvas, these variations, which are much too complex to copy, must be omitted and the spot must be transcribed in terms of an average effect. Not only does the color lose its vivacity; the process also robs the drawing of its spontaneity. And no matter how rich and lively and informative the small sketch was, its exact enlargement will come out thin and somewhat empty. This is even more true when the job is big and the painter is dependent on assistants. Here he is forced, in planning the work, to take account of their limitations. He must simplify his drawing, provide them with firm outlines to follow and simple tones to transcribe, all the time hoping to be able to add subtlety and variety to the drawing and color by repainting the work himself at the very end, which, when the time comes, he is probably much too tired to do. As a result of all this, partly because of the prevalent habit of enlarging from sketches, and even more on account of the simplifications necessary in work which had to be executed with the help of assistants, almost all the mural painters of that time, at any rate all the important official ones, were forced to shun the effects of chiaroscuro and aerial perspective which are the real and proper characteristics of oil painting, and to adopt instead the flat color and linear patterns of the poster.

Such a result followed necessarily from the conception of a mural as a complete small picture later to be blown up to mural size. It could easily have been avoided had the painter gone about his work as if he were simply painting a very large picture, using his sketch as a casual memorandum of images and ideas which would get their full treatment only later on the wall. But with the large official murals of the time, this could not be done, for it was the sketch, not the finished picture, which the painter was selling to the committee. The sketch itself had to be finished enough to convince them. And once a sketch is really finished and set and sold, the ideas it embodies cannot be further developed, and it is impossible to work from it with any freedom.

As one can see, the whole conception is wrong. Mural painting is not a special genre. A mural is only a large, a wall-size, picture, and it can be success-

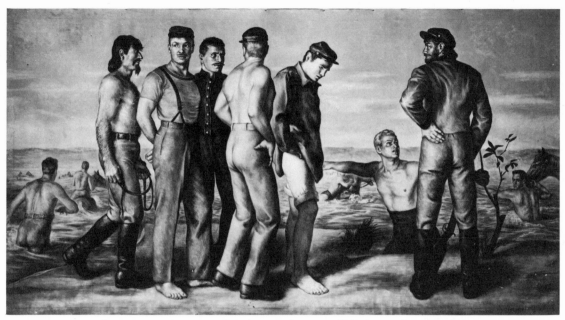

Fig. 24. JARED FRENCH, Jeb Stuart's Rangers. WPA mural, circa 1939.
Parcel Post Office, Richmond, Virginia.

fully executed only by the painter who treats it as such. But painting an integrated picture, large or small, depends either on the painter doing all the work himself, or on having assistants who are trained to work indistinguishably in his style and at his level of skill. This, in the great days of mural painting, was not too difficult, but today it is too much to expect.

Even had these problems been resolved, however, there still remained, especially for an official mural, the problem of subject matter. A picture as big as a mural requires a subject vigorous enough to keep the painter interested during the long time he must take to finish it. In the late 1920s, subject matter for large pictures had grown particularly thin. A little earlier, Rivera had had for subject the preachings of Communism, and Sert the elegant intricacies of a stylistic evocation. Later, in the 1930s, the Work Progress Administration offered its mural painters the theme of the Government Helping the People and had even made room for Jared French's murals in a Virginia post office (Fig. 24) in which the Civil War was brought up to date by using contemporary farm boys from the Civilian Conservation Corps as models for the soldiers. Still later, in the forties, the Abstract painters found as subject for their wall-size pictures the very productive subject of no subject matter at all; today, the Pop painters have taken as their subject the supergrandeurs of the supermarkets and the absurdities of advertising. But the official painters of the late twenties had no comparable theme, and found great difficulty in doing all over again The March of Industry and Progress or The Winning of the West which by this time they had grown quite tired of.

At any rate, none of this tempted me, and I had no desire to excel in the field. I had little time for painting; earning a living took up all of my day, and I was getting nowhere. In the winter of 1928 Virgil Thomson turned up from Paris with the piano score of the opera *Four Saints,* which he was hoping to get produced, performing it at the houses of his friends by singing all the voices, even the choruses, and accompanying himself at the piano. He inspected one of the few pictures I had been able to get done and delivered one of his characteristic oracular pronouncements, always so paradoxical, perceptive, and shocking. He declared that I was an academic painter, which was splendid, he said, because there hadn't been a good one in a long time, and advised me to get back to Paris where living was cheap and where his painter friends would take me on. Soon after, I had a piece of luck, selling a still life to a doctor friend for four hundred and fifty dollars. How the price was fixed, I do not know. Probably that was the sum he had to spare. Immediately I got myself fired by Victor White, to his annoyance and my regret, for we had become very good friends, and I left for Paris. On arriving, I wrote my grandfather and asked his help. He decided that anything I wanted that badly I had better be allowed to do, and coerced the rest of my family into sending me a hundred dollars a month, quite sufficient for living in Paris in those days. And I then set down to attack the problem I had not yet seriously faced—how to paint in oil.

· 5 ·

WARMS AND COLDS

THE KIND OF PAINTING I wished to master was what is called by the very unsatisfactory names of figurative or representational painting—the painting which sets out to give some sort of consistent representation of the visual world we live in. This is a difficult and complicated business, incomparably more complicated, as I had discovered, than drawing. In drawing, all that matters is the ability to see solid form. All the other elements that are so important in painting —color, paint texture, and quality, light, air, and planes of distance—all these can be disregarded as long as what Bernard Berenson called "the tactile values" are preserved. These tactile values—the sculptural, solid forms of things we see, their existence in a space of three dimensions, the motor sensations they arouse in us when our hands explore their surface—do not even have to be explicitly expressed as long as the draftsman has taken them into account. He is not obliged to make the forms in his drawing bulge out in the round. He can draw them flat, without chiaroscuro, in unaccented outline or in cutout shapes. And as long as he has understood the solid masses of his model, his drawing will carry conviction, no matter what graphic idiom he has used.

Another thing that makes drawing simpler: in drawing, one does not have to bother about a background. The object that is drawn is the main consideration, not the space it occupies. It requires no wall or vista behind it to set it off. The subject itself, the nude, the bird, the tree, is quite convincing enough when left by itself with nothing around it but white paper. If necessary, a space behind it can easily be indicated with a sketchy line to suggest a floor or a smudge to simulate a shadow.

Moreover, in making a drawing, pictorial balance is quite easy to achieve. The work is on paper. There is no essential difference between the parts of the paper that have been dirtied and the parts that have been left clean. Both are paper and both have the same weight and substance. So that areas of empty paper can be used to balance the parts which have been worked on, and an empty space which seems overlarge can quickly be taken care of by putting in some slight indication of detail. In fact, compared to painting, drawing is relatively so simple a process that a drawing can almost be defined as a piece of paper which has been dirtied in some places and left clean in others—an accurate enough description, provided only that the man who does the dirtying knows how to see solid form.

Painting, even nonpresentational painting, cannot be defined so baldly. Dirtying a canvas in some places and leaving it clean in others may produce a drawing; it will not produce a painting no matter how well the painter can draw. This is partly a question of balance. Composition in a painting as well as in a drawing depends on the way the various elements—the lights and darks, their shapes and sizes, where they are placed, and so on—are made to balance. In drawing, as I have pointed out, the balance is easy to achieve because the elements are all more or less of the same substance and have comparable weights. Oil painting, on the other hand, has no such built-in unity. Oil paint has immeasurably more weight and substance than the canvas on which it is painted. The two textures are so different in quality that one cannot be used to balance the other. The mechanical regularity of unpainted canvas—even more mechanical when the weave is picked out by a thin wash of color—appears so poor and thin when placed beside the robust variety of a handmade oil paint surface, that one cannot leave large areas of bare or even thinly painted canvas and hope to arrive at anything but an unfinished picture.

This is nevertheless a mistake that almost all young painters make. They have learned in working with pencil and charcoal how to set off a carefully executed head or figure by throwing it into a relief against a sketchy background, and how a small area of detailed work can be used effectively to balance large areas of blank paper. In their inexperience, they will try the same things with paint and canvas. But here, none of this will work. The parts of the picture that are worked over with paint will stick out from the unpainted parts. The slight lines and accents and washes with which they hoped to fill out the thinly painted areas and which would have been quite effective in a drawing, here in a painting have no weight whatever. The only result is that parts of the picture appear labored and other parts unfinished. The various elements are too disparate, and their incompatible weights and textures cannot be pulled into a proper balance.

But all this is relatively unimportant. The major and basic difference between drawing and painting is this: In painting, an object cannot be presented without its background. An object must be shown as if it were in three-dimensional space. Even the standard brown tone around a nineteenth-century portrait head pretends to be a dark well behind the sitter. There are indeed a few paintings of single figures by Manet which have nothing in the background but some dark-brown paint. But even here, the floor on which the figure stands is always carefully represented, so that the brown paint may be taken as an economical attempt to depict the studio wall. In fact, there is almost no exception to the rule: in oil painting, an object must have a background. And more than that, not only must there be space behind it, but the object itself must be painted so that it seems to lie behind the surface of the picture.

That is to say, the picture must have air in it, air whose visible presence, like some transparent jelly in which the objects of the picture are embedded, serves to demonstrate the volume of the space they occupy. Real air, the air in which we ourselves move and breathe, is never perfectly clear. It has a color and a substance, partly from the color of the air itself which is the blue of the sky, and partly from the dust and smoke and water vapor the air contains. The more air there is between us and an object, the more the color of the object is transformed. Dark tones are paled, losing their own color to take on the color of the intervening air. Light tones keep their color better but are nevertheless blued and darkened. In faraway objects, value contrasts and color variations tend to disappear. Their darks and lights are pulled together till the differences of value become almost imperceptible, and all their colors are grayed and blued by the veil through which we see them—with an effect sometimes as theatrically unreal as when in desert country a distant mountain, which we know is nothing but orange-red rock, shines through the clear blue air with the bright pink of a peony.

This effect, the paling and bluing of distant things, is known as aerial perspective. The Greek and Roman painters, who had no conception of geometrical perspective such as we ourselves take for granted, nevertheless understood and used aerial perspective very well. There is, for example, in the Naples Museum, a figure from one of the Pompeian frescoes whose pointing arm is made to recede behind the rest of the body simply by being painted in paler tones than the rest of the figure and with less contrast between its lights and darks, as if the arm were plunged back into a mist. Aerial perspective, like binocular vision, is an essential element in our perception of space, whereas geometrical perspective is largely a matter of convention. There are a great many forms of it and which particular sort a painter employs will depend on which of the conventions his public is accustomed to accept. Aerial perspective, on the other hand, is a primal necessity in painting; neglecting it leads to confused and overdetailed pictures without air or convincing distance. The glassy and unreal brilliance characteristic of Dali and of the Magic Realist painters he influenced comes largely from their voluntary avoidance of aerial perspective, which they replace by an exaggerated use of perspective lines and vanishing points.

Thus, unlike a drawing, a painting must be worked on all over, and also it must have air in it. The most important difference, however, between painting and drawing lies in the means which are used for modeling a form. In drawing, the modeling is done in simple tones of black and gray and white, whereas painters are obliged to deal with what is known to the trade as "warms and colds," a "warm" being a tone that tends toward the red-orange, in contrast to a "cold," which tends toward the blue-green.

In drawing, modeling a form is a simple and straightforward business. Color is not involved. All one needs for presenting a solid form in chiaroscuro is a range of tones, all of the same color, and graded from light to dark. The lightest tone is usually the tone of the clean paper; the darkest is the darkest mark that the chalk, or pencil or ink or whatever one is using, can be made to give. Suppose one is drawing a nude in charcoal. A pale gray will represent the local color of the skin. Tones lighter than this serve to indicate the parts of the body facing the light, and the darker tones are used for the parts in shadow.

In painting, so easy a system cannot be made to serve, even with the simplest subject. Let us take an egg and try to paint it with a series of gradations of the same tone, such as one would use in drawing. We begin by matching the color of the egg shell with a tone of paint. For painting the lights, we lighten this tone with white and for the shadows, we darken it with black. And with the range of tones we have made up in this way we set out to paint the egg. But no matter how accurately we match our tones of paint with the gradations of light and shadow we see on the egg, or how carefully we place and blend them, the egg on the canvas will come out looking very little like the real egg before us. It is simply because the tones we have used in the painting have none of the variety of color to be found in the lights and shadows of the egg itself.

Let us take the egg, then, and try to paint its lights and shadows as they actually appear. The egg we have selected to paint is, say, a light beige. It is lying on a mahogany table near a north window of a room with yellow walls and a white ceiling. We will not bother to mix a tone of paint to match the local color of the shell; we would use too little of it, for the local color of the egg is everywhere modified by the color of the light that falls on it, and none of this illumination is pure white. Here in our particular setup, the brightest light, coming from a north window, will be cold and bluish in tone. The highlights of the egg must then be done in the color that the beige shell will take under a bluish light, which will be some sort of neutral gray. The light reflected from the white ceiling, a little warmer perhaps than the direct light from the window, will make the top of the egg into a slightly warmer gray. The light striking the yellow walls will come back on the egg to tint its middle tones with yellow. And the same light, falling on the mahogany table top, will reflect up on the underneath of the egg as a dark, warm, orange red. The very darkest part of the shadow, which gets less of this up-light, will remain by contrast comparatively cold. Thus, even with such a simple object as an egg, it is not enough to paint the egg alone, or to regard it as an independent entity complete in itself. This one must leave for drawing to do. In painting, an egg must be looked at as if it were a sort of mirror which reflects everything around it, all the lights that fall on it and all the objects in its neighborhood. This is the fundamental device which makes representational painting possible. Only by seeing and recording the visible effects that their surroundings have on the things he is painting, can the painter succeed in making the objects in his picture appear to exist in their own space. This is particularly true for nearby objects.

All this sounds very complicated, and indeed it is. But it can be made much simpler by the use of a trick which Martin Mower, my teacher at Harvard, pointed out. One must think of the subject of a picture as a stage set lit by the usual means of stage lighting—top lights, side lights, footlights, and spots—

and as on a stage, each light of a different color. Suppose we are doing a sunny landscape. Here the top light is blue—it is the sky. There is one spotlight—the sun. The footlights will be the light reflected up from the ground; they will be green if reflected from grass, and orange red if reflected from plowed land. A patch of grass in shadow but exposed to the sky will be bluer than the same grass in sunlight. In shadow, the yellow sunlight is intercepted, and the green is lit by nothing but the blue light from the sky. A white wall in shadow will vary from green and red-orange to purple and blue, depending on whether the lighting at each particular point comes more from grass or ground or sky. Distant objects will follow another rule. Their colors are all governed by the same conventions of stage lighting as the nearby objects. But all the tones will be modi-fied by the intervening air, exactly as if this air were a series of curtains of blue-gray theatrical gauze.

The same trick can be turned on indoor subjects (Col. Fig. 4). A painter's studio, if possible, has north windows, the idea being that if direct sunlight cannot enter, the quality and color of the light will not change unmanageably during the course of the day. In sunny weather north light is blue. Even in cloudy weather, it is relatively cold. The studio furnishings and floor are usually warm in tone, and the walls will also be a warm or neutral gray. Consequently, the lights and highlights on a model posed in such a studio will be cold. The shadows, which are lit by reflections from the floor and furnishings, will be warm. The deepest shadows, which do not receive much of this reflected light, will probably be colder than the middle tones. The flesh of the model, and the clothes she wears, and the chair she sits in as well, will all follow the same sequence—cold lights, warm middle tones, and relatively cold darks. The flesh tones will exhibit an extra complication. Flesh is translucent, and when the light traverses it, as it may in a nostril, on an ear, or in the edge of flesh around a fingernail, the red under the skin comes through as a bright vermillion quite foreign to the sequence. But this, like everything else, must be checked by observation. The sequence I have called normal—cold lights, warm middle tones, and colder darks—will change enormously according to circumstances. In another setting there may be, for example, warm lights, cold middles, warm darks, and cold darker accents. Nevertheless, some consistent series must be found and followed in the painting, not only for the flesh of the figures, but for the clothes they wear, the objects that surround them, and the walls of the room they occupy. Even the distant landscape seen through a window must follow some related series of warms and colds in its painting, though not necessarily the same one; the lighting out-of-doors will be different, and there will be aerial perspective to take into account.

These warm-and-cold sequences are of critical importance in figurative painting. They are the hidden core of its traditions. They are the only means a painter has to endow his picture with an air of reality, to create a space, and to situate the painted objects convincingly within it.

However, it is not at all necessary, possible, or even desirable to transcribe the warms and colds exactly as they occur in nature. Their ramifications are too complex to follow out completely. Nevertheless, they must be looked for and found, even if not precisely copied. As long as they have been seen, they can be treated as one wishes, suppressed till they are nothing but slight differences of browns and grays, as in the work of Boudin or Vuillard, or exaggerated till they become, as in Bonnard and the German Expressionists, violent contrasts of blue and orange. But unless they have been seen and in some way taken care of, the work will not be a painting but a drawing in color. The extraordinary brilliance and clarity of Tiepolo's color, done with almost no bright color at all, comes from the way he keeps the warms and colds which he uses clean and distinct. In the modeling of his figures and draperies and architecture, there is surprisingly little change of value from one tone to another, and all the tones, even those which seem the brightest, clearest reds and blues and yellows, are actually enormously muted, in fact are nothing but earth colors and blue grays. But simply because the warms and colds have been kept sharply separated and unmistakable, the modeling comes out bold and vigorous, and the color sings.

Herein lies Picasso's most striking deficiency as a painter. Perhaps it is a voluntary one. Certainly the pictures he did as a child, the masterful watercolor of his father, for example, in the Malaga Museum, or the early Toulouse-Lautrec–influenced pictures with their striking oppositions of pink and green, show that at one time he knew all about warms and colds. In his later work, however, he makes very little use of them. In paintings like the big Neoclassic nudes of the early twenties, or in the portrait of *Olga Picasso dans un Fauteil* (Fig. 25), the modeling of the flesh is monochromatic, and the color is on the whole reduced to the role of decoration. As a result, these pictures, even though done in a fairly representational manner, have little air or depth in them, and however brilliant the execution, they are more like drawings in colored paint than like paintings in oil. The disregard of warms and colds is even more

Fig. 25. PICASSO, Olga Picasso dans un fauteuil, 1917. *Private collection.*

disturbing in certain of Derain's nudes, where the modeling, done in a mono-chrome of brown and tan, endows the flesh with an unappetizing air of inflated rubber.

There is a diagram we were all shown in school called the color circle (Col. Fig. 5), a chart in which all the bright colors are lined up in order around the rim of a circle, with the duller tones lying inside the circle, and with neutral gray placed at the exact center. In this diagram, the warm and cold colors fall on opposite sides of the circle. The line of separation is a diameter running from the bright yellow at the top, through neutral gray at the center, down to violet. All the colors and all the degraded tones on the blue half, from greenish yellow to blue-violet, are called cold, and everything on the red-orange side from orange-yellow to red-violet, are named the warm tones. But in reality, warm and cold are only relative. Warm and cold operate only as a pair, and a color can be identified as warm or cold only in relation to another color. A blue-green is colder than a green. A vermillion is warmer than a scarlet. One gray can be said to be warmer than another, but the brown of burnt umber will be warmer than either, and this in turn is colder than the brown of burnt sienna. When two tones are of more or less the same relative darkness, which is the warmer and which is the colder is quite easy to decide, even for the untrained eye. A pair of dark browns or two pale grays are simple enough to grade. But when it comes to a pair of degraded tones of which one is light and the other dark, distinguishing warm and cold is not so easy. To tell, for example, whether a tan is warmer or colder than a dark brown, or whether a pale gray is warmer or colder than a dark one, becomes extremely difficult, particularly when the tones one wishes to define are not simple, factual patches of paint, but tones one sees in nature, the tones, for example, of light and shadow on a face or drapery. But this is exactly what one must learn to do if one is to paint them. And this is perhaps the most difficult of all the specialized accomplishments a painter must acquire.

The trick of likening a painting subject to a stage set can be very useful in learning to see these warms and colds in nature. At least it points out to the beginner what must be looked for. Without some sort of guide, such slight differences are likely to be invisible to him. Little by little, however, as his eye is trained by mixing tones of paint and matching them with the objects he is painting, these warms and colds, which at first seemed negligible subleties, begin to stand out and assume their real importance, which is tremendous, for, as I have said before, they are the basis of all representational painting. It is possible

79

not to have mastered them and yet have considerable skill and taste in decorative color. But without their aid it is impossible to make an object seem to exist in air or lie behind the surface of the canvas. And, just as learning to draw depends on training the eye to see solid form, learning to paint depends on training the eye to see and distinguish the warms and colds.

· 6 ·

PARIS AGAIN

CÉZANNE

AND STILL LIFE

LET US LEAVE these abstractions and come back to my own story.

Now, on this second visit to Paris, I was more mature, better prepared to face the problems which oil painting presented, and well aware of my ignorance. I realized only too well that I knew nothing about color; I was even convinced that I had no sense of it. I had no ease in handling oils, for I had not yet acquired that necessary familiarity with the palette which enables a painter to find the tone he needs as automatically as a pianist strikes the right notes on a keyboard. And I still believed, as all students believe whose training has stressed drawing, that somehow or other paintings could be made by tacking drawings together. The guides I had available to me for painting in oil were the three usual ones of the time—Sargent, whose watercolors I had already imitated and whose virtuosity in oil I had always admired; Monet, whom I had encountered through Dr. Ross and his tempered palettes; and Paul Cézanne.

These three names by themselves specify the three sources of instruction available to American painting students in the 1920s—Sargent typifying the conservative virtuoso tradition already becoming old-fashioned; Monet evoking the tradition of Academic Impressionism; and Cézanne standing for the radical, advanced left wing of painting then known as modern art. Sargent's influence was confined for the most part to professional portrait painters and commercial artists; Monet and Impressionism still dominated the solid conservative world of art instruction; while the brighter, younger, and more adventurous of the American painters had already given their allegiance to Cézanne and the school of Paris of which he was the father. In all this, Renoir, Degas, Gauguin, and Van Gogh, enormously celebrated as they were, had little influence. Glackens, of course, was doing marvelous work as a sort of American Renoir, often, to my way of thinking, better than Renoir himself, but he was the only American whom Renoir influenced. Gauguin, with his South Sea Islands, had engendered only inferior imitations, as had Degas's ballet dancers. Van Gogh had greatly influenced Matisse and the Fauves and the German Expressionists, all of whom in their turn were having considerable influence on painters here like Marsden Hartley. But Van Gogh was too near Impressionism to serve as source for painters like myself who were trying to break away from it. As for Matisse himself, and Braque and Picasso as well, it was becoming evident that, admirable as they were, they were essentially mannerists, each busy inventing and exploiting his own recognizable style. They were easy enough to imitate if one wished to appear fashionably modern, but they were all too specialized to serve as guides to fresh discoveries. Cézanne, on the other hand, more flexible and less conscientiously mannered, seemed to show a way out of Impressionism and to provide general principles of painting which could be applied to other than Impressionist subjects.

As a result, Cézanne's influence was as tremendous here in America as it had been in Paris; with this difference, however, that here in America his influence was necessarily indirect, simply because in America the pictures themselves were too difficult to see. Few of them were yet in collections open to the public. And though any number of books about Cézanne were available, the illustrations in them gave only a vague idea of what the pictures themselves were like. The black-and-white illustrations told nothing of the pictures' size or paint quality; even the range of black-and-white values was frequently misrepresented, while the color reproductions, just as today, were all quite false. The texts that accompanied the illustrations seemed a safer guide. At any rate, the writers had themselves seen the pictures. And the descriptions and interpretations and precepts they gave seemed reasonable and easy to follow. The most influential of them all was Clive Bell, with his slogan "significant form." Bell, in this context, was certainly not intending the word *form* to be taken to mean sculptural form. He clearly had in mind the curious fact that the formal elements of a picture, the lines and shapes and colors, can be a source of pleasure in themselves, quite unconnected with the role they play in presenting an image. Significant form, despite its noble ring, is an unfortunate expression, for *form* can mean a geometrical shape or a temporal pattern, as in music, or a three-dimensional solid, as in sculpture, and *significant,* with the primary meaning of meaningful, is here just about as meaningful as *very.* Just the same, equivocal or not, the slogan was adopted as battle cry by the new fashion in criticism, an aesthetic which deprecated all literary content, all subject matter, in a work of art, and based its judgments on the work's formal elements, its lines and shapes and colors and the effect they produce unaided on the spectator. The phrase served as an apology for Cubism—remember the character in a Carl Van Vechten novel who says, pointing to her Metzinger, "I bought that picture because it has significant form"—and came later to be used to justify the completely abstract picture, the picture with no reference whatever to the outside world, a genre which Picasso for one most thoroughly deplored. The slogan's supreme importance as the basic axiom of aesthetics remained unquestioned until the coming of Dada, which questioned every aesthetic value, even the value of art itself.

Significant form had been originally employed by Clive Bell to explain the qualities of Cézanne's pictures. And here, since Cézanne's apples were indeed sculptural, *form* could be mistaken to mean solidity, particularly since Cézanne himself had said that he wished to make of Impressionism something solid like the art of the museums—though by "solid" he certainly had in mind not "sculptural" but "important" or "valuable." Added to this, Cézanne was fond of quoting the well-known academic precepts used by drawing teachers, that all solid forms can be analyzed into the basic ones of cone, cylinder, block, and sphere. And Berenson in writing about Florentine painting had invented the criterion of "tactile values," which the critical world took very seriously indeed. All this together convinced us that Cézanne was uniquely interested in doing some sort of sculpture in paint, and led straight to the cylindrical limbs and ball-round heads exploited by such different painters of the period as Léger and Guy Pène du Bois (Fig. 26)—a mannerism nowhere to be found in Cézanne's own works. I am even convinced that the 1925 taste for the massive and heavy in furniture and decoration, its friezes and statuary in oversimplified modeling and static atti-

Fig. 26. GUY PÈNE DU BOIS, Meditation. *Courtesy The Graham Gallery.*

tudes, with thick ankles and unflexed wrists—even the large, red, meaty, female nudes Picasso was doing at this period, as well as the men's fashions of the time with their skin-tight jackets and elephantine trouser legs—all derive from this widespread misinterpretation of Cézanne.

Nonetheless, even if the School of Paris of the twenties was largely derived from the things found or thought to be found in the painting of Cézanne, Parisian painters had the advantage of being able to consult the pictures themselves. American painters, on the other hand, with only the photographs to guide them, were obliged to be content with the innovations and characteristics which were striking enough for a photograph to show—the diagonal twill brushstroke, for one, which reappears in the work of so many of his followers both here and abroad, or Cézanne's particular device of perspective so useful for filling up a canvas, by which the two sides of a still life are painted from different points of view—a device which is supposed to have been the generating idea of Cubism. Another was Cézanne's way of dealing with the optical illusions which occur when lines intersect or pass behind a shape, his systematic use of distortion by which the outline of a head or an apple would be drawn out of true to compensate for the pull of a line in the background. This use of distortion which he employed for reasons of drawing only, had enormous influence on the painters and led directly to a fashion for the use of distortion for its own sake, a fashion carried to its extreme conclusion in the Picassos of the late twenties—those quite caricatural figures with pinheads and swollen bodies.

I myself was introduced to Cézanne at Harvard, the very year I had begun to draw, by a fellow student, James Mahoney, an ambulance-corps veteran who was enrolled in Baker's celebrated drama course, the 47 Workshop, and who had encountered the works in Paris just after the war. My first real Cézanne I recall seeing in company with Virgil Thomson at a show of French painting in a Boston gallery—a small still life with a few green apples—which I obediently admired and still remember clearly. Led on by Mahoney's enthusiasm, I carefully studied all the books and illustrations I could get hold of, and already in America had painted still lifes on the Cézanne model, arranging compact groupings of fruit on a table top with folds of drapery hung behind for background, and trying to paint everything as sculptural as possible. For this I used a trick in which I had great confidence—painting the retreating edges of a form bluer and colder than they actually were (Cézanne himself drew all his outlines in prussian blue) and exaggerating the red and orange tones in the parts that faced the eye. The theory on which this practice was based I am afraid was a faulty one. It

85

explained that the lense of the eye is not corrected for chromatic aberration; that a spot of blue is brought to focus at a point nearer the retina than a spot of red. And consequently, if one looks at patches of blue and red painted side by side, the red patch will seem to stand out in front of the blue one. Unfortunately, for my particular eye perhaps, this is not true. For example, on the cover of a record album which has red and blue lettering on a black background, the red letters will always seem to me to lie below the surface, while the blue ones float above it —the exact opposite to what the theory predicts. But this effect I had not yet noticed, and besides, the theory was too neat to question. I accepted it as a proven fact and laboriously painted all my edges blue and all advancing planes in red or orange, arriving at quite uninteresting color tonalities and never realizing that the contrary system, of red outlines and blue advancing planes, would probably have worked just as well.

Now, my second time in Paris, I decided that I needed more freedom both in color and handling than any such artificial system could provide. Above all, I needed more ease and speed in working. I knew very well how to draw in chalk or charcoal, but not at all how to draw with a brush in oil. Some sort of practice in virtuoso-style brushwork would certainly free my hand. And as for color, I had been using too many pigments to be able to know what any of them was capable of doing. I found for myself a room to paint in, rather dark, with one large window giving on a court. I got my friends in and made them sit for me in the nude, all in the same pose, seated and facing front, the right shoulder to the window and the left draped in a white turkish towel bathrobe. I painted them on fairly large canvas in almost life size, used for color only white and black, and worked with a large and heavily loaded brush. The results were brilliant and a little shocking, all the more so since the faces were rendered without expression, and the eyes without lights and to the front, making the figures look as inanimate as a set of zombie waxworks and very nude indeed. (My charming concierge on seeing them could not help saying, "*Il y en a, n'est-ce pas, pour tous les goûts.*") By the time I had got around to the fourth of the series, the black-and-white palette had become too strict a limitation, and I began patting some yellow ocher in the white and umber in the black to give a little more warmth to the tones. After this, I turned the same system of harsh lighting, rapid brushwork, and limited palette to still-life subjects, adding a new pigment to my palette only when I could no longer get along without it. By the end of six months, I had acquired a considerable mastery of brushwork and had reintegrated to my use all the pigments.

As far as painting went, the results were disappointing. Only the heads of the four nudes, cut from their bodies and mounted on smaller stretchers, proved to be worth saving. Black-and-white, forthright and resembling, they had something of the urgency of handbills advertising a wanted criminal. But they have long disappeared together with all the others of the time. As for the still lifes, I am glad they are gone. The too brilliant execution, done with a brush that followed the forms, gave a knifelike hardness to the edges, and the violent contrasts of light and dark that I had used in modeling precluded any subtlety of color. I had indeed acquired a certain ease in handling oils and brushes, but everything I did was marred by the crudity inherent in the method. I had learned all I could from Sargent and the virtuoso brush. It was time to reexamine Cézanne and try to learn something about the careful handling of edges, which had been one of his principal preoccupations.

In this last, I believe, lies Cézanne's greatest contributions to the art—his way of beginning a picture by attacking directly the edges of the objects he was painting, using these outlines as the basic framework for his picture, a framework which was never set and fixed, but which could be continuously shifted and adjusted as the painting progressed (Fig. 27). Is it easy to reconstruct from one of his numerous unfinished canvases how he went about it. Let us suppose, to make it as simple as possible, that he was doing a still life with a minimal subject—a peach on a plate on a tabletop. First, he would situate the objects on his canvas, drawing in the outlines, usually, in prussian blue. These outlines, however, were only tentative, a first approximation. Then he would begin the actual painting by laying in his colors in pairs along these outlines, the tone on the inside of the line made up to match the color of the object, say the peach, at a particular point of its edge, while the tone put on the outside of the line would be matched to the color of the background just behind it. Thus, the background and the object lying in front of it would be painted at the same time, as if they were two inseparable things, as indeed they are. In this method, as one can see, the edges become the painter's principal preoccupation, not only the exterior edges of the objects, but also those inner edges within the forms where one value or color merges into another. These oppositions of tone on the two sides of an edge Cézanne considered so important that often, when he felt that they had been sufficiently explored, he was content to stop the picture there and leave the central parts of the objects in bare, unpainted canvas.

The outline—this one must remember—does not exist in nature as an independent thing. The particular shape which an outline assumes depends not only

Fig. 27. PAUL CÉZANNE, Still Life with Apples, 1895–98. Oil on canvas.
Collection, The Museum of Modern Art, New York. Lillie P. Bliss Collection.

on the shape of the object; it depends as well on the point of view from which an object is viewed. We move our head an inch and the shape of the outline changes. Thus, both in drawing and painting, the outline is a convention, a line to be used where it will give the most effect, and which often can be omitted without detracting from the apparent solidity of the form it is supposed to enclose. Only the most innocent beginner starts off by drawing a hard outline and filling it in with paint. The experienced painter knows that his outlines must be kept fluid and loose so that their position, and the position of everything else in the picture, can be shifted about at will as the work progresses. The system Cézanne devised makes all this quite easy. To shift an edge, the painter has only to push into the outline with the tone he has been using for painting the object, or for shifting it in the opposite direction, he cuts into the form of the object with another outline and erases the first with the background tone.

Cézanne's habit of using prussian blue for outlines is responsible for the somewhat drab blue tonality of these still lifes. Ordinarily, the tonality of a picture derives from the color of its darks and middle tones rather than from its light ones. The tonality of the Romantic painters is brown because of their systematic use of brown shadows. A Monet will tell as a blue or lavender or tawny picture, depending on whether its darker tones are blue or lavender or orange. With Cézanne, however, the predominant cold blue of the outlines is not the only reason for his pictures' steely cast. Part of this comes from the prussian blue itself. Prussian blue is the most powerful of all the pigments. Once placed on the palette, it tends to invade everything, especially the light tones. And unless one is very careful indeed, the picture in which it is used will be thrown into a bluish key and come out looking as if it were covered with a pale blue glass. Another and more attractive characteristic of these pictures is their restricted value range. All the tones are close together. Rarely are there deep blacks and never is there anything approaching a pure white. If one places a piece of white paper next to the white in a Cézanne, one is always astonished to find how very dark the lightest tones in the picture actually are.

When I saw how easily Cézanne had avoided the harsh overlighting and brutal transitions which my virtuoso brushwork had led to, and this simply by keeping his values close together and attending to his edges, I turned to him for help. I began doing quite small still lifes in as narrow a range of values as I could manage, watching carefully the changes of value and color at the edges of the forms—where the edge was lighter than the background, where it was darker, and where the two merged and the outline disappeared. I did not realize how closely I was following my teacher, for when Gertrude Stein, seeing a small sketch of mine of a box of kitchen matches and an apple, remarked rather maliciously, "What is that; a Cézanne?" I replied in all innocence, "No, an unfinished picture," an answer which seemed to amuse her a great deal. Just the same, under this new discipline, my painting finally began to work. The pictures, when they were finished, did not at all resemble Cézannes. The small still lifes, in fact, turned out to be quite presentable, and I was at length upon a road which might lead somewhere.

Still life, as a matter of fact, is one of the best disciplines for learning to paint, simply because the subject matter peculiar to it, of inanimate objects, is so easy to control and dominate. But each kind of painting subject has its own built-in problem of composition. In painting flowers, for example, the flowers and the vase present no particular difficulty; the problem is what to do with the empty spaces of a tabletop on which the vase is sitting. The problem in portraiture lies in filling the blank space around the head. With still life, the problem is the background, and in any exposition of still lifes, the most interesting thing, to a painter at least, is how the backgrounds in the pictures have been taken care of. The still-life objects themselves, the apples, fishes, violins, and cans of dog food are easy enough to arrange in harmonious groupings. The question is what to put behind them. Rubens and his school put whole kitchens complete with kitchen maid; the Impressionists presented their fruit and wine glasses as the remains of a dessert left on the dining room table; while Cézanne and Chardin most frequently placed their still-life objects on a table or buffet close up to a wall. But whatever background or setting is used, the space behind the objects must nevertheless have a certain depth. Even in a Cézanne or a Chardin, the wall is shown as lying two or three feet deeper within the picture than the front of the table. Such a shallow recession is too slight to use aerial perspective for explaining it. The only way it can be shown is by the position of one object in front of another and by the perspective lines of the table itself.

If no depth or recession at all is indicated, one gets a special form of still life with a special name, trompe l'oeil. Here the background must be painted as if it were just another of the still-life objects. Harnett's violin and the rough wood door it hangs on are both painted in the same detail and manner. Notice, however, that the violin hangs flat so as to present its broad side to the viewer. Trompe l'oeil works only if the space depicted in the picture is no deeper than three or four inches, so that there is not enough distance between the nearer and the farther details to engage binocular vision. If the violin were presented as if seen end on, the space it occupies is then too deep for the illusion to be produced. And though the picture might still deceive a single and motionless eye, it could no longer deceive the two eyes working together—which is trompe l'oeil's only excuse for existing as a separate class of painting.

My own particular solution to the background problem was not to have any background at all. If the objects fill up the canvas, then there is very little background left to paint. Since I did not wish always to paint small pictures, I was led to enlarge quite arbitrarily the images of the objects I was painting till they were big enough to fill the particular canvas I was using. Thus I was led to produce a series of gigantic vegetables (Fig. 28) and, in particular, eggs (Fig. 29) so monstrous that when they were shown, a visitor was heard to remark, "How they must have hurt the hen!" Just the same, the unexpected magnitude of the objects commanded attention and served to endow the pictures with a certain monumental importance.

The fruits and vegetables which served as models for all this were often very bright in color. This presented another problem. Painting things in very bright color, and at the same time endowing them with high relief as well, is not too easy. One can paint in very bright color indeed as long as the objects can be presented in a flat, head-on light, and one does not have to insist on strong shadows or heavy modeling. This holds for color photography as well. But when the light comes from the side, and when the painter wishes to emphasize the mass of the objects by using a chiaroscuro with marked differences of light and shadow, then to make a painting, or to take a photograph, which has no colors but bright ones, becomes extremely difficult. If one is to paint in chiaroscuro, both dark and light tones are necessary. But a bright pigment is at its brightest at one particular value level only; when it is darkened with black to make a shadow, or mixed with white to make a paler tone, its vivacity is enormously dulled. Also, adding white or black to a pigment completely changes its hue. Vermillion, for example, when darkened with black, becomes a muddy brown, and when it is mixed with white, it loses its orange fire to become a purply pink. Thus, to render a brilliantly colored object with one side lit and the other side in shadow and at the same time use only the brightest colors, to exhibit the object's full solidity and at the same time keep its lights, middle tones, and shadows all at top intensity, becomes almost impossible. It can be managed, but only with many compromises and much ingenuity.

Some of the pictures I painted with this intention were successful, others were less so, and I eventually gave up the attempt, for the effects attained were

Fig. 28. MAURICE GROSSER, Still Life, circa 1938. *Collection Peter Linderwood.*

Fig. 29. MAURICE GROSSER, Eggs, 1950. *Collection Virgil Thomson.*

scarcely worth the effort. After all, bright color itself is not of especial value in a picture. What one wants is the appearance of bright color, which is quite a different thing. The trouble with bright colors is that we possess only a few of them, and these when used pure are always unmistakable. A bright red on a canvas, if it is a red orange, must be either vermillion or cadmium red. If it is a red mauve, it can only be alizarin or madder. No other bright red pigments are permanent or at any rate reputable enough to be in use. The degraded colors, on the other hand, the tones got by mixtures of pigments, are innumerable and their components impossible to identify. Moreover, by proper juxtaposition, these degraded tones can be made to seem as bright as pure ones. A dulled-down blue properly set off by other colors will shine on the canvas as vividly as pure cobalt, providing that no sample of pure cobalt lies near enough to make comparison. And the color harmonies composed of degraded tone are innumerable, whereas the number of color harmonies based on the use of only the bright pigments is limited. That is why the Fauves, who thought to paint in bright colors only, so quickly exhausted the possibilities of the idea, and probably is why Fauvism as a school of painting had so short a life.

The generating ideas behind all this still-life painting of mine seem idiotically simple. But painting in its way is not very different from mathematics or physics, where quite trivial notions are often the cause of the most revolutionary changes. Think, for example, of the enormous extension in mathematical analysis due to the almost simpleminded suspicion that perhaps A times B is not necessarily always the same as B times A. Or the revolution in physics due to the equally simpleminded notion that a foot rule in motion has perhaps not quite the same length as a foot rule lying still. And my two tiny ideas—of paying close attention to the edges, and of doing away with the background problems by enlarging the objects till they filled the canvas—were enough to keep me profitably busy at still-life painting for a number of years. Still life as a genre has perhaps little intrinsic interest for the general public. But for the painter, it is the most fruitful of disciplines, the form of painting least trying on the nervous system and least subject to accidents beyond his control. In landscape painting, there are far too many days of rain and mist, when the light is dirty and distances vanish and the work must be put off till the weather mends. And as for the figure painter, how many exasperated hours is he not forced to pass waiting for an unreliable model. None of this can trouble the easy course of the still-life painter's daily work. Changes of weather bother him little. Each morning finds his sitter already in place waiting for him to begin, perhaps a little more dusty and withered than the day before, but requiring no wages or flattery or entertainment. The art students' silly crack that while there is still life there is still hope is fundamentally exact. And for my own part, even now when I have lost all interest in this sort of painting, whenever there is a new way of putting on paint or a new system of color to explore, I turn back to still life and to that most monumental and exacting and naked of all subjects, a plate of eggs.

At that time in Paris, in the early thirties, the most talked about and promising of the young French painters was Christian Bérard. He, Pavel Tchelitchew, and the two Berman brothers, Léonid and Eugène, made up a group in rebellion against the abstractionism which had dominated European painting since the war. Their manner of painting was as different as possible from the sort of exercises in decoration and composition that abstract painting had by then become. Their romantic and humane subject matter had gained them the title of Neoromantic. The Berman brothers were, and still are today, painters of moody and poetic landscape. Bérard and Tchelitchew painted heads and figures reminiscent of Picasso's "blue period." Tchelitchew I knew slightly through George Antheil. Bérard I knew very well, having come on him through Virgil Thomson, who was one of his close friends and who already owned a small collection of his works— a great many drawings, a sleeping figure, and in particular, a large portrait head which I admired enormously, a somber and not very resembling study in paint and candle wax of a man we all knew named Walter Shaw (Fig. 30). Bérard was quite young then, about my own age, I believe, but was already a formed artist surrounded by an admiring coterie. He was a marvelous and inventive draftsman with sure taste and a perfect sense of decorative color. Plump and round-faced, with a prominent, slightly arched nose, a mouth outlined with a very definitely drawn Cupid's bow, he had not yet acquired the untidy beard and habit of dirt for which he was later famous. We took to one another at once, and, at his suggestion, I painted his portrait. I learned a great deal from him, partly from his pictures and partly from the things he told me about my own work, particularly on the importance of taste and deliberation in the choice of one's subject. Up till then, I had been all too ready to include in a picture anything that happened to lie before my eyes. For a month we saw a great deal of one another. Then, to my regret, I lost his friendship through, I believe, my faulty knowledge of French. I met him at the opening of an exhibition of his drawings, and he asked me how I liked them. I replied, *"BéBé, c'est très chic,"* intending what I thought was the highest praise, not at all understanding the

95

Fig. 30. CHRISTIAN BÉRARD, Portrait of Walter Shaw, 1927. *Collection Virgil Thomson.*

word or realizing that "chic" was the title he was most afraid of meriting. When I called at his house the next day, he was not at home to me, and except at a distance, I never saw him again.

The portrait I did of him, painted in close values and cold blue tones, has disappeared long since in the depths of Alabama. I remember it as a good piece of work. At any rate, it was the beginning of a whole series of portraits, all of friends, which eventually furnished the material for my second Paris show (Figs. 31, 32, 33). The Neoromantic influence in the pictures was unmistakable, not in the painting, which was fairly direct, but in the characterization of the sitters, who were shown as if leading their own lives behind the surface of the canvas, detached from the spectator, attempting neither to charm nor to impose, as if the sitter were quite alone, unaware of his painter and lost in a world of his own.

I remember the show with a certain pleasure, partly because I have never been so consistently successful with portraiture since. The reason is not hard to find. These were friends. Paris in the thirties was a curious place where everyone accomplished a great deal of work but seemed to have leisure as well, and there were always friends around who had time for posing. Imagine finding anyone in New York today with time to come and sit as often as needed and that during the hours when the light is good! Even to find paid sitters is difficult enough. And sitters who pay the painter offer quite a different problem. Here it is the paying client who commands, not the painter. It is the client, in fact, who is painting the portrait and using the painter as a tool to accomplish it. And though I have often painted commissioned portraits which succeeded in pleasing the sitter, I have seldom done one which pleased me enough to wish to put it on show and boast of it as mine.

Fig. 31. MAURICE GROSSER, Portrait of Serban Sidery, 1932. *Whereabouts unknown.*

Fig. 32. MAURICE GROSSER, Portrait of Mrs. Alfred Barr, 1932.
Collection of Mr. and Mrs. Alfred Barr.

Fig. 33. MAURICE GROSSER, Portrait of Prince Leone Massimo, 1932. *Artist's Collection.*

· 7 ·

EXPERIMENTAL METHODS

NONE OF MY PAINTER friends or associates in Paris engaged in much experimentation with out-of-the-way painting methods. Kristians Tonny was a draftsman rather than a painter (Fig. 34). He had been taught to draw by his father, a Dutch painter named Tonny Kristians, and had devised a very pretty way of making drawings by tracing through a piece of paper whose back he had covered with oil paint. But at this time, this was almost the only use he made of paint. Bérard, Tchelitchew (Fig. 35), Léonid, and Eugène Berman, had all learned to paint in oil at the schools they had attended, and none of them seemed to need any other means of expression. Bérard, it is true, at one period used to build up the impasto of his pictures with beeswax from candles, and Tchelitchew did some playing around with gouache, and followed the one-time fashion of dusting the wet paint of his pictures with spangles and sand and even coffee grounds. But I doubt that any of them had ever read a book on paint-

Fig. 34. KRISTIANS TONNY, Pilgrims, 1935. *Courtesy of Wadsworth Atheneum, Hartford.*

Fig. 35. TCHELITCHEW, Prelude to Arabesque, 1934–37. Wash, brush, and ink.
Collection, Museum of Modern Art, New York.
Gift of Tina Marinoff Van Vechten in memory of Carl Van Vechten.

ing techniques or tried to manufacture their own paints. Léonid, to this day, does not seem to know the names of the pigments he is not in the habit of using. All of them bought their painting materials from the most reputable manufacturers and, in general, followed the painting methods they had learned in school.

They were all of them very fine draftsmen and drew all the time. But none of them except Kristians Tonny regarded drawings as anything more than material to be used in the course of making paintings, or as notations of ideas for theatrical costumes and stage sets. Eugène Berman, in particular, possessed innumerable sketch books filled with beautifully executed figures and architectural details, all made during his travels, drawings which he refused either to give away or to sell, and which he kept on hand as source material for his gouaches, stage designs, and paintings.

The fact was that nobody in Paris thought of drawing as an end in itself. Indeed, none of the students at the art classes I myself had attended there, at Julian's, André Lhote's, and so on, seemed to draw particularly well. The academy nudes they turned out had little of the sharp, professional quality that one was accustomed to find in the American schools. Drawings, particularly life-class drawings, unless they were by very famous painters, were not very salable in Paris. And since painting was a profession in which the French students hoped to make a living as well as make a name, there seemed little point in working too hard at one of its less profitable branches. The techniques of watercolor, so assiduously pursued in England and America, were also neglected; there was very little demand in the French picture market for anything but oil. A professional style in oil painting was what the French student sought to acquire. And any knowledge of form gained in life-class drawing was immediately put to use with brushes and paint.

Here in America, on the other hand, painting in oil was by no means the easy and familiar commonplace it was in Paris. Painting materials were expensive in America and proper instruction was hard to find. Consequently, the American student would usually keep on working to perfect his skill in drawing simply because he did not know how to go about learning to paint. And when at length he got around to taking up oil painting, it was likely to seem inordinately difficult. He had been trained to think in terms of line and of black-and-white values. Now he was faced at the same time with the unfamiliar problems of color and with the difficulties inherent in oil paint itself. Oil does not lend itself to a technique based on drawing; oil painting, gone at as if it were an exercise in line and shading, will turn all too quickly into something that looks and feels like oilcloth.

Consequently, a great many young American painters of the time, myself included, were tempted to abandon this respected and exasperating process and to set out in search of some magic formula which would paint all by itself, all of us hoping to discover the perfect painting medium, one which would blend tones as easily as charcoal, pick out details as delicately as a pen, have the covering power that oil exhibits only in thick, unwieldy coats, and retain its freshness of surface even when overworked, as oil will not. After all, why should not some medium of the sort have once existed? The seemingly effortless effects of the old masters could scarcely have been got by skill alone. There must have been some secret preparation which, if found, would render painting as easy and straightforward as drawing.

A student more at home in drawing than in painting would naturally look for something to make paint easier to draw with. Oil paint is far from opaque, and a great deal of it is needed to hide something underneath. White paint, in this respect, is worst of all, and tones made up with white are never dense enough to cover unless they are put down quite thickly or in several coats, one on top of the other. Such bulk of paint does not facilitate the execution of details. Besides, oil paint as it comes from the tube is heavy and viscous. For fine or detailed work, it must be thinned, which further lowers its opacity. Spirits of turpentine and poppy and linseed oils are the usual diluents. But turpentine robs the paint of its luster and its body, and if used to excess, turns oil paint into a sort of inferior form of watercolor with no body or luster at all. The drying oils, linseed and poppy, maintain the paint body better, but at the same time tend to clog up the canvas and produce a greasy paint surface on which subsequent painting takes very badly. There is, however, a painting medium which is neither watery nor greasy and which for this reason was enthusiastically adopted by many American painters of the time.

This was the Marogier medium, named after its inventor, Jacques Marogier, painter, picture restorer, and author of several books in which he describes his discovery as the lost secret of the old masters. Indeed, the medium is not new. It was well known in the nineteenth century under the name of megilp, after a Scotch painter named MacGulip who is supposed to have originated it. It can be bought already prepared, and it can also be made up at home. For this one takes ordinary linseed oil, adds an inch or so of white lead squeezed from the tube, and puts it on the stove to cook—a somewhat dangerous and disagreeable business, for the mixture boils and fumes and stinks and sputters and is all too likely to catch on fire. The result is a black and highly siccative oil. This oil, when it is cool, is mixed with mastic varnish—gum mastic dissolved in spirits of turpentine. The two liquids combine to form a paste, unctuous like thick cold-cream, which is the Marogier medium.

To use it, a tiny bit is applied with a rag to the surface of the canvas one is to paint on, and if one wishes, a little can also be mixed with the paints themselves. The results are dramatic and gratifying. The brush skates over the canvas as if on glass, and all brush strokes, even the thin, unloaded ones, come out crisp and graphic. Slight washes of color, or slight scumbles of opaque paint, can be applied and rubbed and blended together as easily as if they were in chalk or charcoal. And anything can be at once cleaned off the canvas with a rag dipped in a little of the paste—all this without the slightest risk of clogging up the grain of the canvas or producing a greasy surface. And oil paint, which is normally so resistant to painting details and so difficult to blend, is transformed by its help into a most flexible and sensitive instrument for drawing.

I was introduced to the medium by Reginald Marsh (Fig. 36), in his Union Square studio on a hot summer day, who demonstrated its advantages and fluidity by using brown paint mixed with a little of the paste to sketch one of his characteristic tough little shop girls on a panel which had been rubbed in advance with the medium. I asked him whether it took long to dry. "Not long," he said and fetched from the balcony above some other sketches done a few months before. They were still tacky. "It is very hot up there," he said apologetically, which was perfectly true but not very reassuring. The paste he was using, I think, was some he had made himself, and perhaps had not been properly cooked. Later, John Koch (Fig. 37), who was just as enthusiastic about the medium as Marsh had been, and seemed to have no trouble with its drying, offered me a professionally prepared sample. I gratefully accepted and used it in painting a study of some trees, not mixing it with my paints as Marsh had done, but only greasing the surface of my canvas with it before starting. The quality of brush stroke which it gave delighted me—fresh, crisp, and calligraphic, like the brushwork in Chinese painting. A year later, when I judged the picture to be dry, I started to varnish it with a spirit varnish, with dammar gum in spirits of turpentine. At the first touch of the brush, the paint dissolved in the varnish and flowed away. I did not try the Marogier medium again.

I have been told that this was my own fault; that spirit varnishes cannot be used on a picture painted in this medium. One uses instead a coat of the medium itself. This I should be afraid to do. All varnishes are fragile, darken with time, and must eventually be removed and replaced. Any picture of a certain age will

Fig. 36. REGINALD MARSH, Eyes Examined, 1946. *Courtesy Reyn Gallery.*

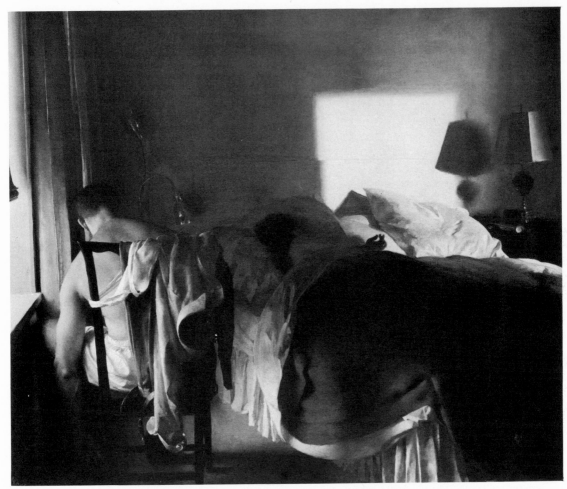

Fig. 37. JOHN KOCH, Morning. *Collection Mr. and Mrs. Prentis C. Hale.*

already have had this done a number of times. In view of this, a painter usually likes to wait at least a year before varnishing, until the paint is dry enough not to be softened or dissolved when varnish is washed over it. In this way, the varnish will lie on top of the paint as a separate and separable film, easy to remove without disturbing the paint underneath. With the Marogier medium, I doubt that this is possible; the substance which acts as varnish also permeates the paint film, and any solvent that would remove the one would dissolve the other as well. Besides this, the two components of the medium, the mastic varnish and the drying oil, are each by themselves of questionable permanence, and I doubt that they become more permanent when combined. At any rate, megilp, the Marogier medium's nineteenth-century prototype, enjoyed in its own time a very dubious reputation.

However this may be, the medium suited Reginald Marsh extremely well. He was essentially a draftsman in paint and not much interested in color. His effective and handsome pictures are actually in an eighteenth-century watercolor style—wash drawings with tints of transparent color imposed on a framework of brown—and not very different, even in subject matter, from the work of the eighteenth-century English watercolorist, Rowlandson. Other painters, working in a more authentic oil-painting style, like Roger Baker or the incredibly skillful John Koch for examples, have found the medium an indispensable aid for producing highly detailed work, and the paintings they have done with it have stood up admirably. I am nevertheless of the opinion that the habitual use of such an aid would tend to turn a painter's attention to drawing and composition and away from color. At any rate, the black-and-white photographs of works done with the Marogier medium frequently seem more imposing than the pictures themselves—a natural enough penalty for painting with this kind of approach.

There is another, earlier Marogier medium which I have also tried—the same black oil mixed with a solution of gum arabic in water. The product is a creamy emulsion, a little of which is to be mixed in each of the pigments on the palette. I prepared some of it and was delighted with the crisp brushstroke and the glossy enamellike surface it gave. I later tried to make it up again but was never able to get the same effects. It was probably a question of exact proportions. Whether it is safe or not I cannot tell. The two pictures I painted using it were sold by a decorator to a client of his own, and I have no way of finding out their present state. But Marogier himself must have some difficulty with the mixture, either in making it up or in its reliability, for it is not mentioned in his later books.

Leaving aside all these trick painting mediums, there is another solution to the difficulties of painting which always occurs to a student overtrained in drawing: Painting a picture would be ever so much simpler if one could begin with drawing and then put in the color afterward. It could then be done in two separate processes, each comparatively easy in itself. First one would draw; then one would color. The Venetians, as I have already pointed out, were known to have worked like this. They began by laying in the composition of their picture in monochrome, with all the drawing more or less complete and all the lights and darks in place. Then, on top of this grisaille framework, they applied their color in the form of glazes and rubbings and scumbles. The seventeenth- and eighteenth-century painters went on doing much the same thing. Even Goya in the nineteenth began his pictures with a black-and-white preparation on which he put his color later, and in these pictures, the cool tone in the flesh is often only some of the gray underpainting left uncovered. There are unfinished pictures by Ingres, like the *Odalisque* in the New York Metropolitan, still in the leaden tones of a preparatory grisaille, which was most certainly intended to be repainted later in full color (Fig. 38).

The underpaintings of Goya and Ingres and the other nineteenth-century painters are apparently in oil. This is supposed to be a dangerous practice and, as I have pointed out in another place, an underpainting in oil is likely to crack if it is not thoroughly dry before it is painted on. Besides, a smooth and detailed underpainting, such as Ingres and some of the other nineteenth-century painters used, takes oil very badly and is apt to give a flat and most unpleasant surface. The underpainting of the Venetians' pictures was certainly not in oil. Anyone who has tried to copy one of them knows that, no matter how skillful the hand, the marvelous and apparently effortless paint quality of say, a Tintoretto (Fig. 39) or a Veronese, cannot be got with present-day oil paint squeezed out of a tube. Quality such as this requires a very different kind of paint, most probably a special paint for underpainting which would dry quickly enough to be worked over at once, but which would somehow stay wet long enough for the separate brush strokes to be blended. Unless tones of paint can be rubbed together on the canvas, transitions from one tone to another can be effected only by the sort of cross-hatchings one finds in steel engravings—a stiff and laborious technique, characteristic of the early tempera paintings, but never found in these Venetian pictures. Besides this, the paint for such an underpainting should not change tone as it dries, and must be loose enough in texture not to clog up and become slick when glazed and overpainted in oil or oil and varnish.

Fig. 38. INGRES, Odalisque in Grissaille. Oil on canvas. *The Metropolitan Museum of Art. Wolfe Fund, 1938.*

Fig. 39. TINTORETTO, An Allegory of Fidelity, Unfinished. Oil on canvas. *The Fogg Art Museum.*

I was at this time back in America, away from the restraining influence of my French painter friends, and the idea of using underpainting to resolve my painting problems seemed very reasonable to me. I put aside my brushes and began to look for this philosopher's stone. Some sort of tempera emulsion seemed the most promising. The trouble with straight egg tempera for underpainting is that it dries at once and changes tone completely in drying. Perhaps it might be possible to find a kind of tempera which would dry slowly enough to permit the paint to be blended on the canvas, and which would also keep the same tone dry as wet. I did not find what I was looking for, but I did come on a kind of tempera that was of considerable use to me.

I was aiming at a water-phase emulsion, that is to say, a combination, like mayonnaise, of oil and water which could be thinned and painted with water and washed out of the brush with water alone. This was probably a fundamental mistake, for all water-phase emulsions set quickly with the evaporation of the water; a paint stroke is dry almost before the next one goes down. Nevertheless, I spent a summer mixing up all the tempera emulsions I thought might possibly work. With each one I painted on a sample card a row of grays graded from black to white. When the row was dry, I would paint another row beside it, matching each dry patch with a spot of fresh wet paint. Since the paint would usually lighten up in drying, this second row would dry out paler than the first. The differences of value in the pairs of tones would then show how much this particular sample would change in drying and in what part of the value range it changed the most. In almost all the sample cards, the dark tones paled considerably in drying; the light and middle tones sometimes paled, sometimes darkened, while a few of the cards showed very little change.

There are two different sorts of tempera emulsions which are known to have been used in painting—one based on egg, usually a mayonnaise of egg and oil and varnish, and the other one based on saponified wax. This is a sort of cream made by boiling chips of beeswax in water to which is added strong ammonia or ammonium carbonate. This cream, mixed with glue, oil, and perhaps varnish, makes up into a painting medium which can be thinned with water and handled like any other tempera paint. In such a mixture, both the glue and the caustic act as emulsifying agents. That is to say, they break down the surface tension of the disparate liquids and enable them to mix. The oil and varnish in the mixture serve to harden the wax. The mysterious Punic wax mentioned by Pliny and Vitruvius in connection with the painting methods of their time may well have been a wax emulsion of this sort. Encaustic paint, known to have been the medium of the Greek and Roman artists, is usually described as sticks of beeswax mixed with pigment, something between sealing wax and colored candles, which would be liquefied with heat and, while still hot and liquid, applied and manipulated with a palette knife. This seems an awkward and improbable way of working. I cannot believe that the crisp details of Pompeian wall painting, or even the later, cruder Coptic mortuary portraits, could have possibly been executed in any such recalcitrant technique. Some sort of water-thinned wax emulsion such as I have described is much more likely. The ancients knew nothing about distillation or volatile solvents and consequently did not have our spirit varnishes. But varnish can be made by dissolving resin in hot drying oil; this is how copal varnish and what is called "amber" varnish are still made. With such a varnish—glue from skins or parchment, and lye from wood ashes used as caustic to saponify the wax —a perfectly good wax-emulsion medium can be made. A similar mixture, of saponified wax, fish glue, dammar varnish and stand oil, I myself found to make an excellent painting medium which changes tone remarkably little in drying and needs no final varnish. If rubbed when dry with a soft cloth, it takes a beautiful eggshell polish. I did not go any further along with this, partly because the paint surface seemed to bruise into darker spots when hit—though these could probably be burnished out with rubbing—and partly because I was more accustomed to the idea of egg. I have always thought, however, that one day I would grind up a set of pigments in a wax emulsion—simply out of curiosity— and find out how they worked, for I have now given up underpainting and trick media and come to believe firmly that oil paint from a reputable manufacturer, used with as little oil or turpentine as possible, is the best and safest paint of all.

I went thoroughly, however, into the emulsions based on egg. These are simple mayonnaises made by using the palette knife to whip into the yellow of an egg whatever oil or varnish mixture one wishes to try. The two best recipes I found were each made with equal quantities of egg yellow and a varnish. The varnish in the first was a commercial waterproof marine varnish; in the second, I used stand oil half and half with dammar gum in turpentine. I settled for the stand oil and dammar mixture because I could not be sure what a commercial product like spar varnish contained. To keep the egg in the mixture from going bad, one must add a little benzoate of soda or some other food preservative. The pigments are ground in water to a stiff paste. Very little grinding is needed; the powders generally come already quite finely ground. For white, I used titanium. It is more opaque than zinc white, and unlike lead white powder, is not poisonous when breathed or rubbed into the skin. The pigment paste is mixed with about an equal bulk of the mayonnaise and bottled in ointment tubes. One tests to see whether the emulsion is holding up by rubbing a brush in the paint and then holding it under a faucet. The paint should wash out immediately and leave the brush with no trace of stickiness. The tubes, if stored in a refrigerator, should keep fairly fresh for several months.

But after all this trouble, my new paints would not work for the sort of underpainting I had envisaged. They dried too fast to be blended on the canvas, and the tones, particularly the dark ones, still lightened up in drying, so that dry tones were still troublesome to match. This could have been easily handled, of course, by working as the old tempera painters did, not from a palette but from a series of pots with tones mixed up in advance. This I could easily have done by making a series of eight or nine grays and bottling them in tubes. But this solution did not occur to me. I was accustomed to painting on an Impressionist system, improvising from blobs of paint squeezed straight from the tubes on to the palette, and using the brush to mix up each separate tone as I came to need it. When handled like this, the new paints were not at all suitable for a Venetian-style underpainting. Even if I had thought of making up the tones in advance, smooth gradations would still be too difficult to get in any such fast-drying medium.

I am told that there is a much simpler method than anything I tried for getting a satisfactory underpainting—working with plain oil colors mixed half and half with casein paint and thinned with turpentine. The mixture, I am assured, dries hard and rapidly even when put on thick, all the while staying wet long enough to be worked into. I hesitate to endorse it because I myself have never tried it. And actually, I never needed to, for I found that with my tempera paints I had a marvelous way of establishing the *mise en page* of a picture. In fact, the new paints made the work of beginning a picture so simple that they solved all my problems of placement and composition and many of my problems of color as well.

Instead of beginning with a carefully worked-out underpainting in grisaille as the Venetians are said to have done, I would take a complete palette of the tempera colors, all of the pigments I would later use in oils, and begin to splash them on as one would do in watercolor, but with the advantage over watercolor that with these paints every slip could be immediately corrected. The tempera set almost at once, and once it was dry, a subsequent coat of paint did not disturb it at all. Anything could be changed about at will, colors and values could be altered, objects shifted from one place to another, erased or added, and in no time at all, I had my picture all laid out on canvas, a rough but complete frame-work with everything in its place, in the proper color and at the proper color value. At this point, I would put the tempera tubes back in the paint box and carry on the modeling of form and the refinements of detail in the more maneu-verable medium of oil.

This was especially useful because at that time I was trying to paint in very bright color. A pigment ground in tempera always appears more brilliant than when it is ground in oil. Cobalt blue, in particular, is so much brighter that it seems a different pigment altogether. In addition to this, tempera is usually painted on a pure white ground, which in itself is conducive to painting in high key. Thus, the colors of the underpaintings come out so much brighter than the oil paint one puts on top of them that the painter is forced to keep his oil tones as clean and bright as possible in order to try to match them.

In doing this, however, one must be careful not to leave any of the tempera paint uncovered. Everything must be gone over with the oils. Tempera changes very little as it grows older. For this reason, in the restoration of an injured pic-ture, the portions to be repainted are usually done in an egg paint which will not darken with age. Oil paint, on the other hand, changes considerably as it grows older, yellowing and darkening, and all the while gaining richness and depth of color. Consequently, any bit of tempera left showing in the picture will eventually stand out as an inconsistently brighter and paler spot.

In a technique of this sort, there is always great danger of the paint cracking and peeling. Whether or not this happens depends largely on the painting ground, on the priming coat which prepares the raw board or canvas to take the tempera. The painting ground must hold firmly to the canvas, and the tempera in its turn hold firmly to the painting ground. Otherwise, the oil paint on top of this, when it shrinks as it does in drying, will pull everything off. This is exactly the same effect one finds on painted wood left exposed to the weather, where an upper coat has contracted and slid and split to expose the underneath coat in an alligator-skin pattern, and where, if this coat itself is not firmly attached to the wood, the whole paint film pulls up in concave flakes like dried mud in a swamp bottom. In fact, an oil-paint film contracts so strongly in drying that the wooden panel of a picture, which has warped, can often be pulled back into true simply by painting its back with a large cross in fat oil paint.

A gesso ground, made of whiting in thin glue applied hot and in successive coats, is considered perfectly safe. At any rate it is the ground on which the old tempera painters always worked. It holds tempera firmly, and if it turns out to be too absorbent for easy painting, it can be rendered less thirsty with a thin coat of glue or gelatin. Gesso, however, is generally considered too brittle a ground to use on canvas, too easily cracked if the canvas is dented, and the books advise one to use it only on a rigid support like a panel. But as for gesso panels, or for that matter, any sort of panel at all, I find them highly impractical. They cannot be rolled up, as canvas for pictures can, and consequently are difficult to travel with. Big ones, if they are wood, are unmanageably heavy and unbelievably expensive. Composition board and plywood panels are cheaper, but when a corner breaks off as so frequently happens—panels are always getting dropped—it cannot be repaired. And as for small panels, they may be cheap and safe and handy, but they have the disadvantage that some prospective client is sure to look at the back of the picture and complain that it is not on canvas. More serious, however, is that when a picture is painted on a panel, an injury to it is very troublesome to mend. If a painting on canvas is torn, or the canvas rots, or the paint film begins to flake, it is a fairly simple business for a restorer to glue the picture onto a fresh canvas, or even to remove the old canvas from the back of the painting and replace it by a new one. But if the injured picture is painted on a panel, the back of the panel must be planed down and rasped and sanded until all the wood is completely removed and the ground on which the picture is painted is itself laid bare—a much more difficult job.

However, gesso when properly prepared is probably not as brittle as it is said to be. The painter Edward Melcarth has used gesso for many years (See Fig. 56), even on very large canvases, as a ground for painting in oil and varnish on an oil casein underpainting. These gesso canvases, he tells me, can be rolled up for shipping and storage without any danger of cracking. The books usually advise priming canvas with a half-chalk ground made by mixing boiled linseed with the hot glue-and-whiting gesso preparation. This may possibly be safer than straight gesso and more flexible, however it is not nearly as white, it yellows even more with age, and when put on thick, develops cracks. Commercial canvas, made up for oil painting and with an oil-base primer, will not do at all as a ground for tempera. It is too fat and nonabsorbent to hold the tempera, which is certain to peel off.

Considering the experimental nature of my tempera process, it surprises me that any of the work I did with it has stood up. Most of the still lifes, nevertheless, are still in good shape except for some cracking in the darks. Such cracking was to be expected. Dark tones, particularly the slow-drying blacks and madders, are always liable to pull and crack, even in straight oil painting. On the other hand, a whole group of portraits that I painted at the same time and with the same homemade paints are now in a ruinous state. These, for economy I suppose, were all done on masonite panels injudiciously primed with a commercial flat white oil paint. Either the wall paint itself has gone to pieces, or it contained varnish and hence was too slick and nonabsorbent to hold the tempera. Whatever the cause, the paint on all of them has flaked and powdered irreparably. And since they were all painted on tough masonite, they cannot be saved by being relined. I should have known better.

My greatest mistake, however, and the one I most regret, was made in the portrait of a doctor friend. This was not a commission; it was a picture painted for our mutual pleasure, and imprudently executed in a new painting medium I had just invented, a medium I believed to be based on a new and valuable and revolutionary principle.

First, each pigment one was to use was ground separately in a heavy, waterproof spar varnish, using as little of the varnish as possible so as to make the stiffest possible paste. This paste was then emulsified with egg yolk; the resulting mayonnaise, thinned a little with water, was bottled in a tube to be used like any other water-phase tempera. The pigments made up in this way, first ground in varnish and then emulsified, did not dry out as brilliant and luminous as in regular tempera. They had the rich and heavy tone of pigments ground in oil. But the paint itself worked beautifully and did not change tone at all in drying. This was to be expected. Each of the pigment particles was coated with water-proof varnish. The water used to thin the mayonnaise could not get at them. They were wet with varnish, not with water, and there was no reason for them to dry out paler as the water evaporated.

The doctor's picture was begun with the new paints and finished as usual in oil. It came out rich in color and was extremely successful both as a picture and as a likeness. The fact that the underpainting did not change in drying made the execution very easy.

A month later, the picture began to crack. My marvelous new formula was not holding to the ground. The oil paint, shrinking as it always does in drying, was pulling the underpainting into cracks. I filled them up. Next month there were more cracks, and more and more. Shortly after this, the paint began to darken. Today, the picture is a network of splits and creases and wrinkles, and so dark that one can scarcely perceive an image.

I have been told that the rigidity of the spar varnish when dry is the reason why my picture cracked; that with a more flexible varnish the formula would

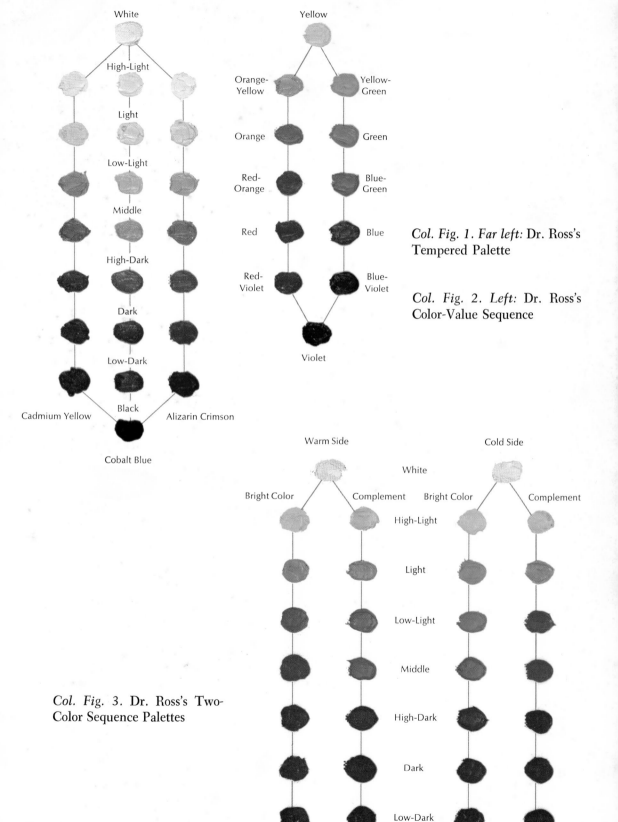

White

High-Light

Light

Low-Light

Middle

High-Dark

Dark

Low-Dark

Black

Cadmium Yellow   Alizarin Crimson

Cobalt Blue

Yellow

Orange-Yellow   Yellow-Green

Orange   Green

Red-Orange   Blue-Green

Red   Blue

Red-Violet   Blue-Violet

Violet

Col. Fig. 1. Far left: Dr. Ross's Tempered Palette

Col. Fig. 2. Left: Dr. Ross's Color-Value Sequence

Col. Fig. 3. Dr. Ross's Two-Color Sequence Palettes

Warm Side   Cold Side

Bright Color   Complement   White   Bright Color   Complement

High-Light

Light

Low-Light

Middle

High-Dark

Dark

Low-Dark

Black

Col. Fig. 4. RENÉ BOUCHÉ, Elsa Maxwell. *Collection Mrs. René Bouché.*

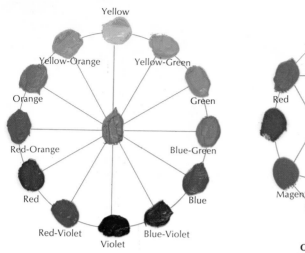

Col. Fig. 5. Munsell Color Circle,
Subtractive Mixtures

Col. Fig. 6. The Impressionist Color
Circle, Additive Mixtures

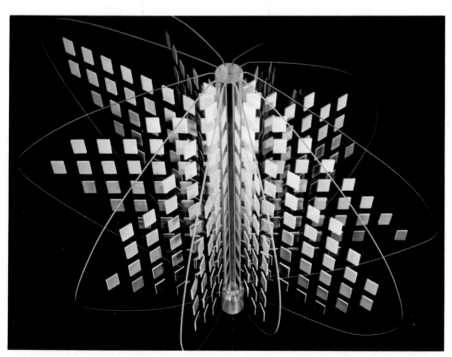

Col. Fig. 7. The Munsell Color Solid. *Courtesy U.S. Department of Commerce.*
National Bureau of Standards.

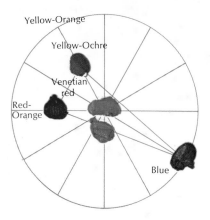

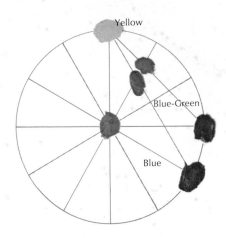

Col. Fig. 8. Geometric Representation of
Mixing Blues

Col. Fig. 9. Geometric Representation of
Mixing Greens

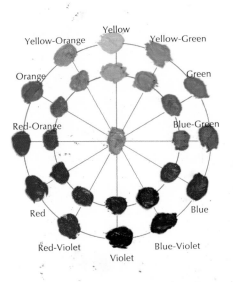

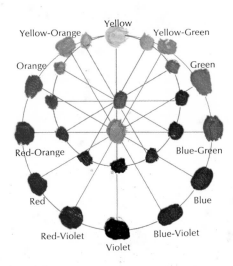

Col. Fig. 10. Geometric Representation of
Muted Colors

Col. Fig. 11. Geometric Representation of
Color Tonality

probably have worked. But even with this improvement, my invention would not have been safe. Each pigment particle was saturated and coated with varnish. And when the varnish darkened with age, as all varnishes do, the paint itself would also have blackened. All this, as one can see, is a problem for a chemist, not for a working painter.

This, of course, is the real trouble with all such experimental painting methods and homemade recipes. The painter has not the training, or the laboratory equipment either, which would permit him to standardize his processes or to be sure of the materials he is working with. Besides, he keeps no notes on what he has done. And when an experiment goes wrong, it will take him some twenty years to find it out, much too late for him to derive any profit from it, for he can learn of his errors only through the irreparable evidence of a ruined picture.

I myself was luckier than I deserved to be. My more ordinary tempera paints, for which, after all, I had a certain justification from tradition, gave me little trouble except when I used them on a ground where they would not hold, and I continued to make use of them for some six or seven years. At length, however, I discovered that I no longer was dependent on them for setting up a picture on canvas; this I could now do quite as rapidly with plain oil paint and turpentine. By then, also, I was no longer interested in trying to paint in the most vivid colors possible, for which the tempera paints had been so great a help. At that point I gave up tempera entirely and went back to straight oil. And except for four or five small still lifes done in the new acrylics, I have used nothing but straight oil paint since.

These new acrylics are a water-working emulsion paint made on a plastic-resin base. Of all the available water-working paints, they are the easiest to use. They spread and cover easily, dry and set at once—with the evaporation of the water—and change tone very little in drying. They are useful both for large, flat canvases with areas of uniform color and for working in the tempera style, in which forms are modeled by cross-hatching. The acrylics have the great advantage that they can be painted on any clean, slightly absorbent surface, like paper or raw canvas or raw wood, a thing which cannot be done with either oil or tempera. If the raw canvas proves too absorbent and slows down the work, this is easily remedied by priming it with a coat or two of acrylic white. A layer of acrylic paint, when it is dry, is not disturbed or softened by fresh paint put on top of it. In fact, the successive coats combine to form a homogeneous film, and there is no danger at all of the paint lifting or cracking. The acrylic medium itself is white and clear, not yellow like oil. Consequently the blue pigments ground in it are a great deal brighter than in oil. As for the reds, oranges, and purples, the manufacturers offer a whole gamut of brilliant new pigments, unavailable in oil and unlisted in any of the standard works on artists' materials, and which one can only hope are permanent. The paint surface obtained is flat, like gouache or poster color. Varnishing with a little of the acrylic medium gives something of an eggshell finish. A heavy gel medium is available which serves to slow down the drying and gives the paint a little more body and gloss. And if one mixes this gel with the colors, they can be blended and worked almost as freely as if they were oils.

Unfortunately not nearly as easily. Although the dark tones of the paints keep their value fairly well in drying, the pale tones darken considerably, which renders working and modeling in the pale color ranges extremely difficult. Using the acrylic paints with a gel medium, I have painted still lifes that cannot be told from oils, except for the somewhat more brilliant reds and purples. But it takes so much longer to do that it is scarcely worth the effort. Their greatest inconvenience here is that one cannot mix up a tone and keep it aside on the palette for later use as one is accustomed to do in oils. The paint squeezed out of the tube hardens and becomes insoluble almost at once, even when used with the gel medium, and each tone has to be mixed up fresh each time it is needed, which means a considerable loss of both time and patience. And even with the gel medium to give it extra body, the blobs of paint flatten out in drying and one can never achieve the rich impasto surface which one is accustomed to get in oils. Besides this, acrylic is probably incompatible with oil, and if painted on an oil-painted surface may well when dry pull off in a rubbery sheet just as it does when painted on a nonabsorbent surface like glass or porcelain.

The manufacturers claim on the other hand, that oil on top of acrylic is quite safe, that acrylic can be used like tempera for a preparatory underpainting to be finished in oil, and that in particular, acrylic white applied like gesso to raw canvas makes a most satisfactory ground for oil painting. One hopes this claim is true, for acrylic is much tougher than gesso, is much simpler to apply, and is so flexible that it does not come off even when the canvas is creased or twisted. I myself have frequently used it as a ground for oils with, as yet, no bad results except on one occasion. A paint merchant whom I assumed to be expert in the matter told me that if one wished to make sure that the oil paint would stick to the acrylic base, one should first treat the base with a preparatory coat of a plastic varnish. I took his advice and varnished the whole acrylic ground with the varnish he had sold me. The picture, when finished, happened to get creased in shipping. Either the oil did not stick to the plastic varnish or the varnish did not remain attached to the acrylic ground, for the paint film broke along the crease to peel in ribbons.

Ralph Mayer, the great authority on artists' paints and methods, says that an acrylic-paint layer remains flexible for a very long time, whereas the oil-paint layer on top of it becomes in drying much more brittle; thus the bond between the two layers is not too secure, and the oil paint may eventually crack and flake off. And Mayer is rather of the opinion that acrylic as a ground for oil had best be avoided simply because the medium has still not yet been in use long enough for anyone to know what actually will happen.

In dealing with any experimental process such as this, the painter is at a grave disadvantage. With new products such as the acrylics, he has only the manufacturer's say-so to depend on. Even when working with more familiar things, he is still more or less in the dark. The sure and tested recipes which once constituted the traditions of his profession, the knowledge of what to use and how materials behave, is now for the most part lost. Whatever technical information he possesses comes to him, not as a set of practical working instructions, but as a collection of unassessed hints and clues, untested suppositions amassed by scholars and exposed in such encyclopedic compendiums of technical possibilities as those of Döerner, Tocqué, and Mayer, hints and clues which are nevertheless intriguing enough to plunge the painter incontinent into experiment. I myself who have been as guilty as the rest, now take the stand like a reformed drunkard to protest that such experimentation, fun as it may be and valuable as it may sometimes prove, is, on the whole, immoral. Pictures are valuable objects, worth the high prices paid for them. Their continued existence, as well as the ways of seeing they preserve, are much too important to be entrusted to chance. A good painter may work with impossible brushes, a filthy paint box, and a palette loaded down with geological accretions of dried and scabrous paint. But he will buy his paint from the most reputable manufacturer he can find and paint on the most beautiful canvas he can obtain. And unless he considers his work to be a joke at the public's expense, he will not stick gumdrops on his pictures in the name of novelty, nor will he entrust his future renown to untried materials, no matter how well they are advertised.

Looking back at my own work, and at the pictures done by experimental methods, with paints and canvases and painting mediums I made up myself, some of them have held up quite well; some of them have not held up at all. On the

---

other hand, the pictures I painted with oil and turpentine, on properly prepared canvas and with paints got from reputable manufacturers, these pictures have never changed at all. And I am driven to the conclusion that if a painter wishes his pictures to last, he must avoid all trick ways of painting and use only the most reliable materials. But this is easier said than done.

· 8 ·

OIL PAINTS
AND HOW TO
MAKE THEM

IT WAS IN Paris that I first learned to be wary of color manufacturers. On the Quai Voltaire, around the corner from where I lived, was the outlet shop of a well-known brand of paints. Its show window displayed a color chart which continued never to be changed despite the fact that every color in it, even the supposedly immutable red earths and ochers, had spoiled and darkened. Such unexpected candor was very persuasive. It implied that all artists' colors were inevitably fugitive, that this merchant alone was honest enough to admit it, and that consequently, the paints he offered must be honest too. I yielded and regretted. Only the color chart was honest, not the colors. The colors themselves were so miserably adulterated that the pictures I used them on began to darken as soon as they were painted. Christian Bérard, to whom I appealed, took me to his own color merchant, Lefebvre-Foinet, an old and reputable house with a long tradition of reliability. It is, in fact, a beautiful Foinet canvas which one sees exposed in the unpainted spots of Cézanne's pictures. And the Foinet *blanc d'argent* is still better, whiter, and more opaque than any other brand of white lead I know.

In America, when I returned there in the middle thirties, Foinet colors were very expensive and very hard to find. Compared to them, however, none of the American brands seemed very good, and I decided to try to make paints myself. This turned out to be quite easy, especially since I had at hand the necessary tools and materials, already acquired for making tempera.

Oil paint is nothing but powdered pigment mixed with a drying oil—that is to say, one of the vegetable oils which, when exposed to air, oxidizes and polymerizes to become a horny and insoluble film. There are any number of these oils but only three are usually considered suitable for artists' use—linseed, poppy seed, and walnut. Linseed is the commonest and easiest to obtain. Poppy oil is paler in color but dries more slowly. Color manufacturers often employ it because it gives a whiter white, and because the tubes of paint made with it are less likely to dry up before they are sold. Walnut oil, recommended by Leonardo, who gives a recipe in his notebooks for making it, was not to be found in Alabama, where I was then living, and I have never got around to trying it. It is said to dry well but also to go rancid quickly in the tube. It is much esteemed in France as a salad oil—perhaps because it is rare and expensive—despite its strong and, to me, disagreeable taste. The directions I give here are for linseed oil, which is the most easily available, for the raw oil, not the boiled variety.

One starts off with the best oil one can find, the top grade known as cold pressed, if possible. Even this should be washed by being shaken up in a jug of water, allowed to sit and separate, the water changed, and shaken up again. After several bouts of this, the clear oil which rises to the top is siphoned off and the layer of scum at the bottom discarded. This is easier to do if one has the sort of separating funnel chemists use for such operations. The oil should come out pale in color. It can be further bleached by leaving it in a stoppered bottle in the sun.

For grinding paint, one needs a palette knife, a muller, and a square plate of glass twenty or so inches across. A muller looks like a squat glass paperweight with a handle projecting from the top, and the bottom flat for grinding. It should measure at least four inches in diameter. A bigger one is still better. It is not a common article of commerce, but one can usually be found at some artists' supply house. My first was made for me by a local glass-cutter who cemented three disks of plate glass together and fitted a wooden trowel handle to a bolt stuck through the top one.

The plate glass grinding slab must have its surface roughened to give it a grain which will hold the pigment. The glass-cutter's shop can do this, or one can grind the polish off oneself with water and a little emery powder, bearing down and pushing with the muller till all the shine is gone from the glass. To make the paint, a couple of tablespoons of pigment powder is heaped on the slab and a little oil is added, enough to mix up with the knife to a thick paste. Then, using the muller, one rubs out the lumps, pushing the paste around the plate till all the particles disappear and the muller slides easily over the glass. When the pigment no longer "sings" under the stroke, the paste is scraped together in a pile. If it is too thick, a little oil is added; if too thin and liquid, which is more likely, one adds pigment and grinds some more. When the paste has acquired the right consistency—*buttery* is the word usually used to describe it—it is slid with the help of the knife into the open end of a tin ointment tube. One goes on grinding pigment and oil together until enough paint has been made to fill the tube within an inch of its open end. The end is sealed by pressing the sides together and giving them a triple fold, and the tube is labeled with a smear of the color it contains. Ointment tubes come in several sizes; the two ounce size is the most useful. They can usually be found at a wholesale drug company if the art stores do not have them.

For the working painter, all this is very useful knowledge. Paints made at home will probably be of better quality than their commercial equivalents; they will contain pure pigment and no adulterants, which is more than can be said of almost all the current brands. Certainly they will be less expensive. A tube of cobalt blue from a reputable manufacturer costs $2 or $3 at least, whereas a whole pound of the pigment, which grinds up to make more than a dozen tubes, costs today in New York only $9.70. Besides this, the paints are surprisingly easy to make. The pigments come already quite finely ground; very little additional grinding is needed, only enough to incorporate the powder with the oil and to rub the paint out smooth. A couple of days work is generally enough for preparing a year's supply.

Certain of the pigments, however, do not grind up so easily; white lead and cobalt blue in particular. White lead in powder is coarse and grainy, the particles tough and resistant to grinding. Only with excessive labor can they be reduced to a paint that will cover properly. Besides this, white lead is a cumulative poison.

The dust is dangerous to breathe. Even in the form of oil paint, it should be handled as little as possible for fear of getting it in the mouth or into cuts in the skin. Indeed, it is preferable not to attempt to grind it but to settle for some good manufactured brand of which there are some very good ones, much better than one has the patience to make at home.

Cobalt blue is also tedious to grind, but it is well worth the effort, for in this case the homemade paint is incomparably better than the commercial product. The difficulty with cobalt lies in the amount of labor it takes to work the powder into the oil, and the disproportionate bulk of the light-weight powder that a very small quantity of oil will wet. One begins with a little pyramid of pigment on the slab, adds some oil, and starts mixing them together with the knife. As the oil penetrates, the pale blue powder, all the while remaining a powder, takes on a darker hue. Then the powder clumps together into granulations. Under the pressure of the muller, the granulations mass together and turn into a stiff, unwieldy paste. Presently the paste begins to liquefy and, as the grinding continues, becomes a watery soup. More pigment must be added. Instantly, the soup is again a granular powder which, under the muller, again slowly thins into a watery liquid. More pigment must be added and the grinding repeated, this several times before the magna acquires enough consistency to use. It takes an unbelievable quantity of powder and a very tiresome amount of grinding to fill a single tube.

I suspect that the manufacturers of artists' colors all hesitate to use this much of the expensive pigment and this much labor, especially since oil plus a little cobalt to color it, and the wax or filler to give it body, will grind up into a paint indistinguishable—until one begins to use it—from a paint thickened with pigment alone. At any rate, I have never been able to find a tube of manufactured cobalt which possessed enough tinting strength to be of any use in painting, whereas cobalt paint ground at home and properly loaded with pigment has almost as much tinting strength as ultramarine.

Ultramarine blue, that is to say the artificial ultramarine pigment, which is the only form of it current today, is also a little difficult to make into paint. The pigment is an impalpable powder. Mixed with oil, it runs like molasses. No matter how much pigment is added, it still remains liquid, never acquiring the consistency of paint until, at a certain point, it turns into an unmanageable blue putty. Alizarin red and lamp black, which also come as finely divided powders, behave in a similar way. Actually, there is no objection to using them in that form, except that such semiliquid paint runs all over the palette. If one wishes a more paintlike consistency, a little beeswax softened to a paste with turpentine can be added. Only little is needed, not enough to affect the tinting strength and probably not enough to impair the toughness of the paint film, As for lamp black, however, the paint made out of it dries so badly that I can see no reason for ever using it. Ivory black, made of calcined ivory chips, is a warmer, pleasanter black and a much better drier. Mars black, an artificial iron oxide, is perhaps preferable to either. It is not as deep a black as either lamp or ivory, but it mixes up to a proper consistency of paint and dries solidly and quickly.

Of all the painter's colors, white is the most important and the most consumed. It is the basic ingredient of almost every tone. There are three whites commonly used in oil: zinc oxide, titanium dioxide, and lead carbonate.

Zinc white is a fairly recent addition to the palette. It appeared on the market in the latter part of the nineteenth century and for a while threatened to displace the traditional white artist's pigment, which was lead. It is more stable chemically than lead in that it is not darkened, as lead is, by sulphur fumes. It proved particularly useful in watercolor, where, under the name of chinese white, it replaced both the white lead and the powdered chalk which had been previously used as body colors, neither of which are at all satisfactory in a water medium. Chalk mixed with water loses its opacity only to retain it as it dries, so that tones made up with chalk are very dark when wet and dry very pale. And white lead, when not protected from the sulphur fumes present in the air, turns into black lead sulfide. It was precisely for this misapplied reason—that lead is undependable in watercolor—that drove white lead out of fashion in oils and brought zinc in.

Zinc ground in oil, however, has little to recommend it. It dries badly and covers badly. Tones made up with zinc white, if they are to hide anything underneath, must be put on very thick. And the thicker they are, the longer they take to dry, so that pictures painted with zinc for white remain wet and sticky for a long time. Zinc, in fact, dries a great deal slower than any of the other pigments except black and alizarin, and when it is employed, the different rates of drying of the different layers of paint are likely to cause cracks. Zinc's only legitimate use in oil painting, as far as I can judge, is in a technique known as "wet into wet," where fresh paint is worked into paint which has remained wet from the previous sittings, and where nothing is allowed to dry till the picture is finished—a method of painting very little employed today.

Lead white, on the other hand, dries quickly and well. When it is used in painting, anything put down one day is quite dry enough to paint over the next.

Mixed with the other pigments, it equalizes their rates of drying and minimizes the danger of cracking. Unlike zinc, which is brittle, the paint film lead produces is tough and flexible. It has incomparably more covering power than zinc; tones mixed up with lead may be used a great deal thinner and will still cover. Lead, when it is ground in oil, does not darken as it does when used as water-color. The oil film around the pigment particles is quite enough to protect them from the sulphur in the air. For proof of lead's reliability, one has only to go to a museum and look at any of the pictures painted before the middle of the nine-teenth century. All were painted with lead; lead was the only white pigment used till then for either oil or tempera.

Titanium, the newest of the whites, came into use only some thirty or forty years ago. It is more opaque and covers better than lead, so much better that pictures painted with titanium can usually be distinguished in an exhibition by their lighter tone. Titanium is the perfect white for watercolor or tempera. In oil, it shares zinc's disadvantage of drying badly, and needs the addition of a drier to make it harden at a reasonable rate. Its paint film lacks the toughness and flexibility of lead, and it is prone to "chalk," to dry to a dusty, powdery surface as if the white powder were working loose from the oil binder. For this reason, I hesitate to use it, particularly since in certain pictures of mine, in which I used titanium, the white seems to have come up to the surface through the other pigments, and everything has paled and grayed and lost its color. On the whole, I suspect that if one wishes to take advantage of titanium's marvelous opacity, it is better to use it mixed with lead and thus combine the good qualities of both pigments, the drying power and toughness of lead with titanium's extra density. Titanium is so much whiter and more opaque than lead that even if one does not employ it as the basic white for painting, one generally likes to have a tube of it at hand to use for highlights and white accents.

Almost as indispensable as the whites are the earth colors, both the natural ones like the ochers, umbers, and siennas, and the mars colors, which are the artificially prepared equivalents. The earth colors range from sandy yellow to brown and from burnt orange through brick red to violet. All are reputed safe and are extremely useful. Each painter has his particular favorites. Mine are pale yellow ocher, indian red, and something called half-burned yellow ocher, a red-clay-colored pigment which I find to be of great help in landscape. Raw sienna, a transparent brownish yellow, also very useful, is said to darken. I have never found it to do so, but if one is afraid of it, it can be replaced by a similar pigment known as italian earth, reputed not to have this disability. Raw umber, a cold dark brown, and burnt umber, a warm one, contain manganese, which acts as a drier. They dry very rapidly, change tone in drying, and may prove difficult to match with wet color. I find them quite unnecessary. Much prettier browns, richer and more transparent than the umbers, can be got by mixing burnt sienna with either prussian blue or thalo blue. Burnt sienna with prussian blue is in fact the mixture employed by those nineteenth-century painters who wished to approximate the tone, and avoid the use, of mummy and asphaltum, those most beautiful of browns and most treacherous of pigments. For mixing browns and grays, both of the siennas, because they are transparent, are invaluable. Raw sienna with thalo blue gives wonderful deep greens, and burnt sienna with ultramarine and white furnishes a complete range of warm and cold grays.

The earth reds—english, venetian, puzzuoli, burnt ocher, and so on—I myself seldom seem to use. They are for the most part quite opaque and with great tinting strength, and mixed with white turn much more toward the violet than one expects. On the other hand, the purple hematite colors—indian red and caput mortuum—I find very useful indeed. Terre verte, a natural green earth, comes in all shades from sage to apple. It is useful only in watercolor or tempera. Terre verte, as I have pointed out, was the standard pigment for underpainting flesh in all the traditional tempera and fresco techniques. In oil, it is thin and transparent, and has too little tinting strength to be of any use. In this particular color range, its modern equivalent, opaque chrome oxide, is incomparably more serviceable because of its greater tinting strength.

There are four blue pigments in common use today—ultramarine, cobalt, thalo, and cerulean. Thalo, or monastral blue, came into use quite recently, some twenty years ago. Thalo and monastral are only trade names; its real name is phthalocyanine. It is an organic compound closely resembling the hemoglobin of the blood. It is quite permanent, an intense, transparent, greenish-blue pigment of enormous tinting strength, so powerful that as it comes straight from the tube, it can be mistaken for black. It has exactly the same hue as prussian blue, which it resembles in every way except that it is considered safer and is considerably more intense and vivid a color. Like prussian blue, it has so much tinting strength that, unless one is very careful, it will invade and stain everything else on the palette. I find it a little difficult to use pure; few of the bright blues I wish to paint seem to lie in the blue-green range. But its depth, transparency, and intensity of hue make it invaluable for mixtures, even for mixing purples, which is surprising, considering its greenish cast.

Cerulean is an opaque pigment, paler than the other blues, which because it is opaque behaves somewhat differently in mixtures, giving a rather more airy quality. It is a little greener than cobalt but not as green as thalo. It is a solid and permanent but by no means necessary color that can usually be replaced by cobalt. Cobalt and ultramarine are more or less alike. Both are bright and both transparent, but ultramarine has a more purplish cast and greater tinting strength. Cobalt, when properly prepared, is one of the most versatile and dependable of all the colors. Ultramarine, on the other hand, beautiful as it is, enjoys a reputation for solidity which, I suspect, the form of it we have today no longer deserves.

The ultramarine of the old masters was a mineral pigment made by pulverizing lapis lazuli, a rare and semiprecious jewel stone, and separating out the blue. The pigment was absolutely dependable both in oil and tempera and extremely expensive, so expensive that in the Middle Ages, when it was to be used in a picture, it was not furnished by the painter but supplied by the client as an extra. Gradually the supply of lapis was exhausted and the color became impossible to obtain. In the eighteenth century, it was replaced by the newly discovered prussian blue, and then later, in the nineteenth century, by the newly discovered cobalt.

In the middle of the nineteenth century, a way was found to synthesize ultramarine, and the pigment became again available to painters. Its synthetic form, Guimet's blue, is a somewhat complicated compound of aluminum and sulphur, and chemically identical to the blue extracted from lapis. But whereas the granules of real ultramarine, derived from crushed stone, are relatively coarse, the pigment particles of the synthetic blue are microscopic. As one knows, the smaller the particles of a substance the greater surface it offers to chemical action. And the minute particles of artificial ultramarine are probably more sensitive than the coarser granules of the real pigment to any acidity of the oil they are ground in. At any rate, the ultramarine blues of Titian and Tintoretto have stood up magnificently, whereas the synthetic ultramarine which Renoir used shows up dull and tarnished in his pictures. The same thing has happened to the ultramarine blue in pictures of my own done less than thirty years ago. If artificial ultramarine could be obtained in a coarser grind, it probably would be safe enough. But as it is, I prefer not to use it. Though beautiful and serviceable, it is not indispensable.

None of this, however, is certain. It is possible that the tarnishing of artificial ultramarine comes more from the yellowing of the oil it is ground in than from any vice in the pigment itself. The vermillion we have today, on the other hand, is without question treacherous. The vermillion used in the pictures of the old masters was apparently a perfectly safe color and has stood up without change in both tempera and oil. The vermillion we ourselves possess does not stand up. Why, I do not know. Perhaps the vermillion of the old masters was really cinnabar, a naturally occurring mineral, and possibly more stable than the artificially prepared mercuric sulfide we have today. I have also been told that mercuric sulfide has two forms, one red and the other black, different in color but chemically identical, and that exposure to light may turn one form into the other. And it may be that our methods of manufacture favor this transformation. But whatever the cause may be, it still remains that the vermillion in the older pictures is as bright as it ever was, whereas the vermillion we have today begins to blacken almost as soon as it is painted. This is a pity, for the cadmium reds we use as substitute are nowhere near as brilliant. On the other hand, these cadmium pigments are completely reliable. A reasonably bright cadmium scarlet, though rare, can usually be found, and in the yellows, the cadmiums offer a full range of the brightest hues going from pale citron to red orange. As for zinc yellow, strontium yellow, and the chromes, there is no excuse for using them. Most of them are unstable and none of them are brighter than the cadmiums.

Naples yellow is a soft, warm, muted yellow without enormous tinting strength, but of great opacity and invaluable in landscape. We were brought up to regard it with suspicion, probably because it is a lead compound. It has nevertheless remained unchanged in the pictures of the old masters who used it extensively; it was by far the safest clear yellow they possessed. And I myself have used it for many years and never had any trouble with it.

As for the green pigments, there are four good solid ones: viridian, opaque chrome oxide, thalo (or monastral) green, and baryte green. The best advice I can give about all of them is that, for painting green, they should be used as little as possible. And as for thalo green, it never should be used at all. Thalo is a deep, intense, transparent, bluish green, of the same hue as viridian but much stronger, in fact, so strong and vivid that it will stick out like luminous paint in any picture where it is used. It is particularly troublesome in pictures viewed under electric light, which for some reason renders the pigment even more vivid still. Viridian, though quieter in tone, should also be used with caution; the greens obtained by mixing viridian with cadmium yellow—which are the greens usually employed for grass and foliage by painters new to landscape— are particularly harsh and garish. The unpleasant spinach greens in the landscapes which Manet did under Impressionist influence are probably this mixture.

131

Green is a very difficult color to render, though I believe that the trouble it gives to beginners, and to a great many experienced painters as well, is largely a question of semantics. The word *green* is a name held in common by half the colors in the color circle. Everything from chartreuse to turquoise is lumped together as green, when as a matter of fact, if one consults the additive mixture color circle (Col. Fig. 6), one will find that yellow green and blue green are as far apart as mauve and orange. Thus, there are a great many more different greens than the beginner can recognize, simply because he has no names for them. He thinks of them all as green, makes no distinction among them, and paints them all alike. Added to this, the greens in nature are usually less vivid than the beginner thinks. Even sunlit foliage is rarely brighter than the moss green of opaque chrome oxide. The brightest greens in a landscape can generally be rendered by mixtures of blue and yellow, and the duller ones by black and yellow, or blue and yellow ocher or raw sienna.

Viridian, however, if too green for grass, is very useful in painting flesh, and with cadmium scarlet, mixes up to make a fine if costly black. Baryte green is not well known. It is a pale, bright, opaque, bluish green, the exact tone of the beautiful but poisonous and unstable paris, or veronese, or emerald green, which it replaces. It is very useful for skies and for green-painted objects in a landscape, like shutters or boats.

As one can see from the list above, the painters today have enough safe and permanent pigments to render two-thirds of the color circle—the part going from blue through green and yellow to orange red—in tones as bright as any to be found in nature. The other third of the color circle is not so easy. The sequence of the reds and purples, from scarlet to purplish blue, is impossible to render with any sort of brilliance except for a couple of isolated hues. A bright orange red can be got by using vermillion or cadmium red, and one can get a bright ruby red by glazing alizarin crimson over white. But vermillion or cadmium red mixed, or even glazed, with alizarin gives only muddy tones, much less brilliant than either of the parent colors. And alizarin lightened with white loses both its intensity and its characteristic hue, to become incomparably duller and a great deal more purplish than when put on as a transparent wash. As for the mauves and purples, there are scarcely any bright ones which are safe to use. Pale cobalt violet, an opaque mauve-lavender, is intense and reasonably solid. But even this bright color mixed with alizarin does not make up into a properly bright red-violet. And the purples made by mixing alizarin and ultramarine are not really bright at all. A number of new reds and mauves, for the most part transparent lakes (i.e., dye colors transformed into pigments) are now available in the acrylic paints. They are not yet well enough known or well enough proved to have been accepted into common use. Perhaps they will help, though what one really needs for the red-purple range are some new opaque pigments. According to present-day color theory, two opaque pigments, say a red and a violet, whose mixture, because they are opaque, is partly additive, will give a more luminous mauve than one can get with a transparent red and violet, whose mixture, because they are transparent, is necessarily subtractive. But more of this later.

Let me summarize by making a palette out of the most useful colors: First, lead white and mars black or ivory black. Then the earth colors—yellow ocher, burnt and raw sienna, and venetian and indian red. For the bright yellows and reds, we have the cadmiums—cadmium yellow, orange, and red—and alizarin crimson. For greens, there are viridian and opaque chrome oxide. And for blues, cobalt and thalo. With naples yellow added, this makes sixteen. Many still can be omitted. Brilliant sun-lit landscapes can be painted with only white, black, a blue, and a few earth colors, and any Tiepolo can be copied with the same palette plus naples yellow. As I have pointed out before, brilliance of color does not depend on the use of brilliant pigments. It depends on proper contrasts of warm and cold and on keeping each tone clean.

· 9 ·

COLOR THEORY

THEORIES OF HARMONY are invaluable to composers and to performing musicians. Theories of color, on the other hand, useful as they are to physicists, are seldom taken very seriously by the painters, who, for the most part, are convinced that in working with color, no theory can replace a well-trained eye. Most painters, just the same, have learned something about color theory at school and presumably have profited by it. What they were taught, and what is still being taught in the art schools today, is essentially the old eighteenth-century theory of primaries, corrected and extended by material derived from Impressionism. A great deal of this has been discredited by discoveries made in work on color photography. But discredited or not, it still remains useful for pointing out in a rough way how the colors behave. There is no way of going into color theory without a certain amount of professional jargon, but I will try to make the little I cannot avoid using as inoffensive as possible.

Gamboge, ultramarine, and carmine were the three brightest pigments available in the eighteenth century. Gamboge (i.e., Cambodia) was the highly purgative gum of a South Asian tree, a bright, clear, transparent yellow, fairly permanent in watercolor but difficult to use in oils on account of its gummy nature. Real ultramarine, which I have described before, was a beautiful bright blue made from a crushed lapis lazuli. And carmine was a vivid scarlet, intense and fugitive, extracted from the dried bodies of a species of insect infesting a Mexican cactus. Since the yellow, blue, and red of this particular set of pigments were the brightest colors to be had, it was natural to suppose that they were the only bright colors possible, and the particular tones of yellow, blue, and red exhibited by this set of pigments were accepted as the basic colors from which all other colors could be made and because of this were named the primaries. The orange, green, and purple made by mixing two of the primaries were found to be duller than the parent hues and so were christened the secondaries. Mixing secondaries produced the tertiary colors—red-brown, slate-blue, and olive. Each primary had a secondary as complement; that is to say that mixing a primary and a secondary (like blue with orange, or red with green) would produce gray. Each secondary had also a tertiary as complement—for orange, the complement is slate-blue, for purple, olive, and so on.

In the nineteenth century, with the discovery of the aniline dyes and other bright dyes and pigments, the notion that red, blue, and yellow were the only possible primaries had to be given up. The secondary colors could no longer be considered necessarily duller than the primaries by any law of nature, because orange, green, and violet dyes had been found which were quite as vivid as carmine and ultramarine. And it had to be admitted that any color, providing that it was bright, could be taken as a primary. One could think of all the hues as equally intense and imagine them arranged in order on the rim of a circle, each hue blending imperceptibly into the next. Within the circle could be placed the degraded tones, also merging into one another and fading to gray at the center. Pairs of complements, like red and green, fell directly across from one another at the opposite ends of a diameter. And any three colors occupying the vertexes of an inscribed equilateral triangle would serve as a set of primaries. This diagram was known as the Munsell Color Circle (See Col. Fig. 5).

A further refinement was then made, one connected with the discoveries which led to Impressionism. It was found that there were two ways of mixing color, and that the same two colors mixed would come out quite differently depending on whether the two tones had been combined in the form of paints or in the form of colored lights. Everyone knew that mixing blue and yellow paints gave green, and it was something of a surprise to find that if a disk, with one half painted blue and the other half yellow, was spun rapidly, the hue produced by the blurring of the two colors would not be green at all; it would be gray. It was explained that blue paint appears blue because it absorbs and cancels out the red part of the white light that falls on it, and reflects back to the eye the indigo, blue, and green parts, which the eye adds together and sees as blue. In the same way, yellow paint absorbs the blue part of the light and reflects only the red and yellow and green parts. Now, when blue and yellow paints are mixed, the colors act as if their component parts were subtracted one from another. The indigo, blue, and green components of the blue paint are subtracted from the red, yellow, and green components of the yellow paint. Thus, red, yellow, blue, and indigo are all canceled out, and nothing comes through except that part of the spectrum which both the paints reflect, which is green.

On the other hand, when blue and yellow are mixed as beams of light, or as dots stippled on a canvas, or as colors whirled on a disk, what the eye receives is the sum of all the hues which each paint by itself reflects. Thus, the red, yellow, and green lights, which the yellow paint reflects, are added to the green, blue, and indigo lights, which the blue paint reflects, and the result of the sum is white or gray. Mixtures of paint were thus termed subtractive mixtures, and mixtures of lights, additive.

In these new additive mixtures, the pairing of the complements is quite different from what takes place in the familiar subtractive ones. Here yellow, when mixed with violet, which is its normal complement, produces a pink. To make a gray, yellow must be mixed with blue instead. In the same way, the complement of green is not the familiar red; it is mauve or magenta. Thus, to deal with mixtures of lights, a new sort of color circle had to be set up (Col. Fig. 6), where all the hues from yellow, through orange, red, and violet, to blue are squeezed onto one side of the circle, and the other side contains nothing but greens, beginning with chartreuse and going on through turquoise. In this additive-mixture circle, the two sets of primaries used in color photography for negatives and prints—yellow, cyan-blue, and magenta, and the complementary triad, indigo, red, and yellow green—come out as the apex points of two intersecting triangles (See Col. Fig. 6). The color-film primaries, of course, have much more precise designation than these vague color names. They are dyes, each with measurable absorption bands in particular regions of the spectrum. The painter can still safely ignore them, for few of them are yet permanent for his uses.

The color theory I encountered at Harvard had also attempted to treat color as an objective and measurable thing, and this with considerable ingenuity. But it succeeded less well than the technicians at Kodak because it failed to take into account the vagueness inherent in the names of colors. According to its teachings, a tone of color, both of an object in nature and of a paint on the palette, could be broken down into three basic factors named "value," "hue," and "saturation," each of which could be measured and written down. And from these notes, without any other information whatever, the tone of color could be exactly reconstituted. The first of these factors, value, or lightness, denoted how light or dark the tone is. It was measured on a scale going from white to black. Our notation had a scale of seven steps: highlight, light, low-light, middle, high-dark, dark, and low-dark, each step indicated for brevity by its initials. The next factor, hue, or chroma, associated the tone with one of the twelve color names: yellow, yellow orange, orange, and so on, these also indicated by initials. The twelve names formed the circumference of a Munsell Color Circle, each name lying opposite its complement. As in the Munsell circle, the center of the circle represented gray, and a point on the rim stood for a color at its highest intensity, so that a tone's saturation, how intense a color it is, how much or how little it is grayed, could be shown by a position on the spoke which joined the name of the color to the center point, and was to be measured from 1, for pure color, to 0 for gray. Thus, any shade of color whatever could be described by three written symbols. A brick red in this notation would be referred to as a red-orange at half saturation and at middle value, and could be written down as RO ½ M, a dark bottle green would be G ⅓ D, and the brightest scarlet possible would be written as R/RV HD, where R/RV represented a point on the rim between red and red violet. With the aid of this system of shorthand to jot down color tones on a drawing made from nature, one was supposed to be able to paint a finished picture in complete and accurate color without going out of the studio, a system of painting all too reminiscent of a system used by a young man who, not too long ago, asked my help. "I have been painting the *Last Supper*," he said, "and one of my most important tubes has given out. Would you mind mixing me up a No. 48?"

The system taught at Harvard was scarcely as naïve as this, and had the weight of considerable authority behind it. In fact, the Fogg Museum library possessed a color dictionary built on such a system, a massive and expensive volume which pretended to contain samples of all possible shades of color. And there was on exhibition in our classroom a "color solid" (Col. Fig. 7) looking very like a piece of abstract sculpture by a Russian Constructivist, which was intended to give a concrete picture of how the color tones were to be classified in three-dimensional form. The vertical axis of the object was formed by the value series with black at the bottom and white at the top, and a cross section of the solid taken perpendicular to the axis at any value level would show by its shape the intensity of color possible to each of the hues at that particular shade of darkness.

Just the same, logical as the system sounds, I do not believe that a working painter could get much good out of it, even as a system of mnemonics. I doubt even that a painter using the same notes twice in succession would come out with pictures at all alike in color. Color is by no means as simple as the theory would suppose, and painting in full color requires more information than the notation can be made to contain. The trouble lies with the factor "hue." The names of the hues that make up the rim of the color circle are all, except for violet, the names we give to specific parts of the visible spectrum. But a name associated with a part of the spectrum is far from enough to describe the characteristics either of a color tone we come upon in nature or of a pigment which we use in painting. And since we paint with pigments and not with spectrum lines, this is a very serious fault indeed.

In fact, the color which a pigment or an object exhibits, can no more be the result of a single frequency of light than can a note struck on the piano come out as a single musical pitch. To the contrary, the color of a pigment is a very elaborate chord of frequencies, much too elaborate to be represented by a single point position on a spectrum band. Indeed, monochromatic light, which can be thus represented, is so deficient in color potentiality that anything viewed by it loses all its color and is reduced to tones of gray. There used to be near Chattanooga an automobile underpass illuminated by some sort of sodium-vapor electric lights, which were of course monochromatic, and I remember how startling it always was on entering it to see the bright red motorcycle I rode change suddenly to a shade of dirty tan. If a pigment could be found which reflected nothing but the narrow portion of the spectrum which salt gives out when heated, it would indeed be yellow, but it would have a heavy, dark, sad tone, and when mixed with blue would give black, not green. If a yellow is to be bright, it must do exactly the opposite of this and reflect a great deal of the spectrum, in fact practically all of it except the blue.

Thus, to say that a pigment has a predominance in a particular region of the spectrum, to call it simply yellow or green, is scarcely enough to describe it. The only way a pigment can be described properly is by a spectrophotometer, a laboratory instrument which measures the amount of light a pigment reflects at each point of the spectrum, and from this draws a characteristic curve (Fig. 40A) which is the pigment's individual signature. These spectrophotometric curves furnish such a complete description of the pigment's character that they can be used to determine which pigments, and in what proportions, have gone into the making of a sample shade of paint. This is of course of little interest to the painters. But it is quite important to the color manufacturers. A spot of repaint on an automobile, for example, a spot which matches perfectly by daylight, will not match when seen under another sort of illumination unless it has been made up with exactly the same pigments as the original color. All this, of course, renders color catalogs such as the Munsell color dictionary quite useless for any sort of exact identification of the color of paints and fabrics. The sample color chips of the catalog are made with mixtures of dyes, which are certainly not the same dyes and pigments used in the paints and fabrics to be matched, so that the chip which matches the color of something under one light will be very unlikely to match it under another.

So, contrary to what one has generally been taught, a brilliant pigment is characterized not by a peak in its spectrum but by a gap. The spectrophotometric curve of an intense red pigment, for example, will show a broad hump at the red end which extends to include some of the orange and some of the yellow. There will be another hump at the blue end, and between the humps— in the green region—there will be a valley. The brilliance of a red pigment depends exactly on how little of the green it reflects, so that how intensely red the pigment is will be shown in the curve by the depth of the valley in the green region. The width of the red and blue humps taken together indicates the pigment's luminosity, how clear and luminous it is, while the profile and placement of the humps define the pigment's color character and show how it behaves in a mixture. The mixture, say, of a red and a yellow paint will usually give an orange, but how luminous and intense an orange it will be depends on how much light both of the pigments reflect in the orange region. In fact, if the spectrum curve of either the red or the yellow pigment did not extend into the orange zone, mixing them would give black, not orange. And as for the variety of possible colors, each having a different character but all with the same hue, think of a bed of red zinnias, each a flaming red and each red different. The two relatively stable red pigments the painter has—cadmium red and alizarin crimson —cannot be put together in any way which could forge such flamboyant signatures (Fig. 40B).

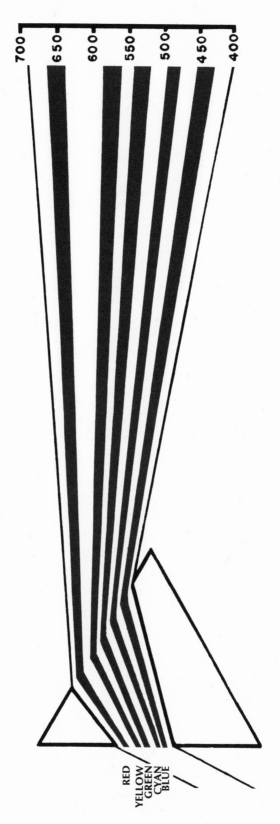

Fig. 40A. A prism separates white light into its components. This is due to the fact that the velocity of light through transparent media depends on its wavelength.

ALIZARINE RED

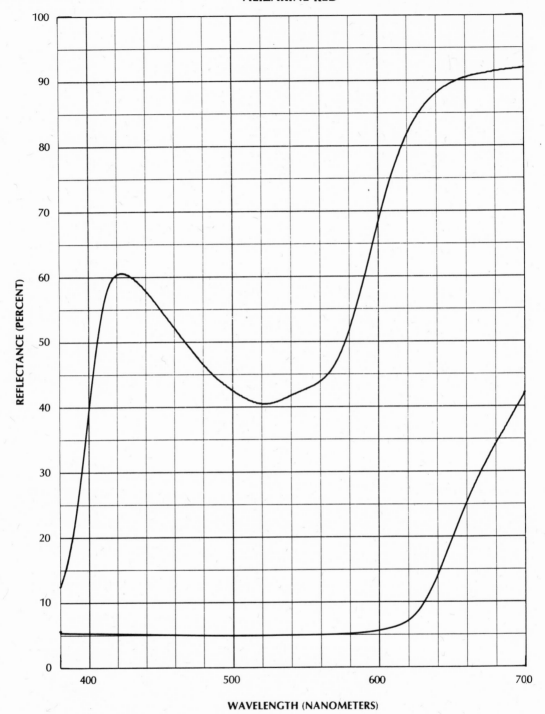

Fig. 40B. Spectrophotometric Curves. *Courtesy Imperial Color Division of Hercules Incorporated.*

VIRIDINE GREEN

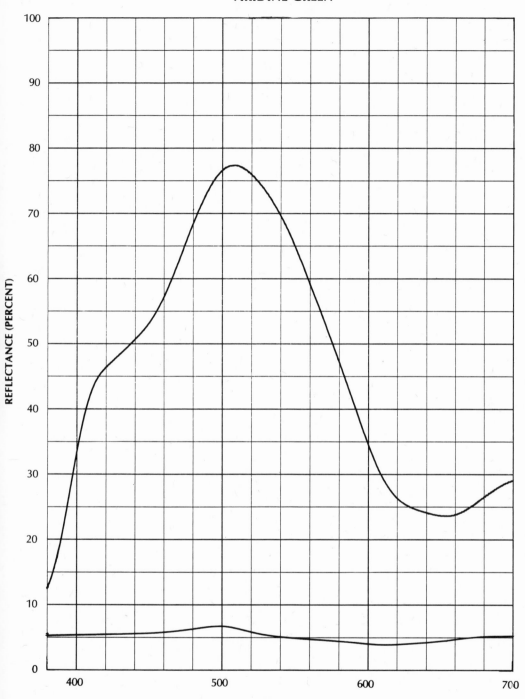

REFLECTANCE (PERCENT)

WAVELENGTH (NANOMETERS)

PHTHALOCYANINE BLUE

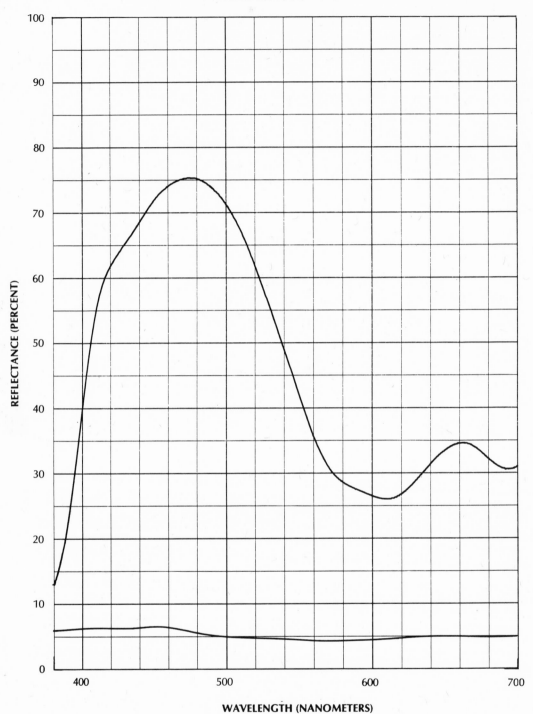

REFLECTANCE (PERCENT)

WAVELENGTH (NANOMETERS)

144

ULTRAMARINE BLUE

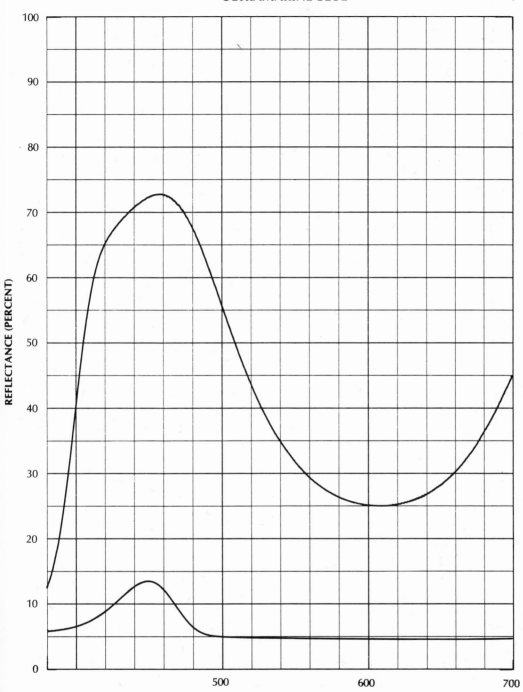

REFLECTANCE (PERCENT)

WAVELENGTH (NANOMETERS)

CADMIUM YELLOW

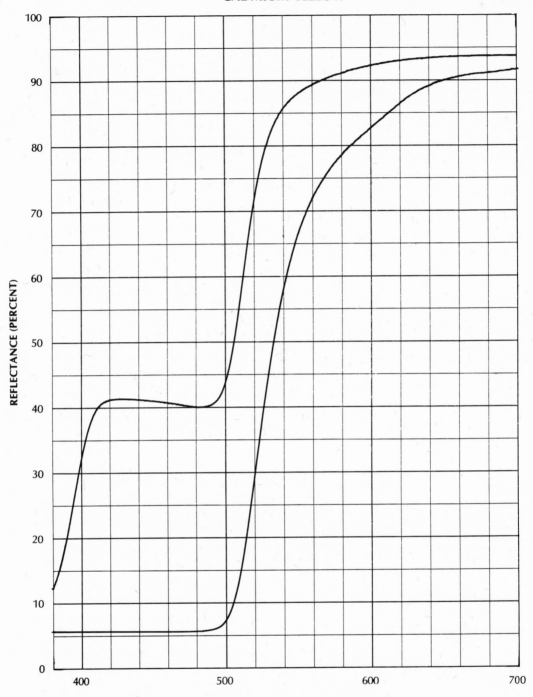

CADMIUM MEDIUM RED

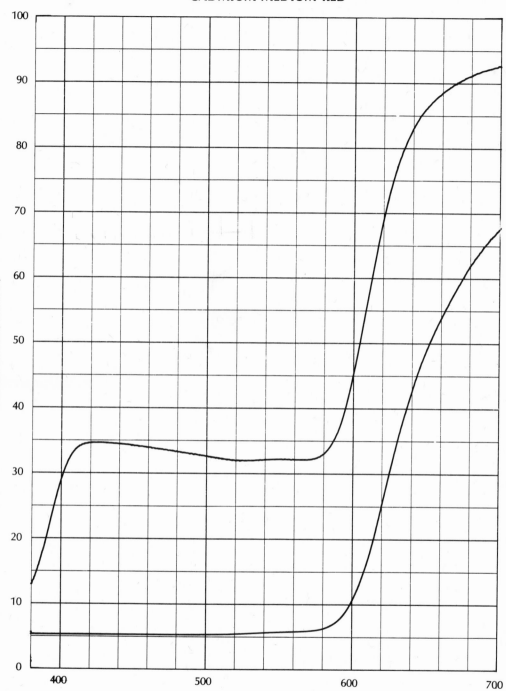

WAVELENGTH (NANOMETERS)

147

I must point out, however, that many flowers owe their vibrant color to something more than the unassisted brilliance of their coloring matter. They are not only bright; they are fluorescent as well. That is to say, their petals can take in the high-frequency ultraviolet light invisible to our eyes and reflect it back in the visible range, reduced in pitch to blue or red or orange. Thus a red flower, say, is able to reflect more of the red than the light which illuminates it actually contains. This is the explanation also for the bright and rather horrid new reds and chartreuse greens that suddenly began to appear in sweaters and on billboards some seven or eight years ago. The dyes used in them are fluorescent. They reflect more color than the light which falls on them would seem to warrant, with the result that they appear too bright for their surroundings, as if they were shining, like luminous paint, by an inside source of energy.

As one can see, the nineteenth-century notion of hue—that the hue, or chroma, of a color can be treated as if it were a point on the rim of a color circle—is much too elementary to account for how colors actually behave. Neither the pigments nor the colors in nature will fit into such a scheme. Nevertheless, let us suppose, for the sake of argument, that there did exist a set of strictly monochromatic pigments, pigments which fitted precisely the separate parts of the spectrum indicated by one of the color names, each pigment reflecting light in the region of its particular hue and nowhere else. If such a set of pigments could be found, they would be impossible to paint with for this reason: The color which is produced when two pigments are mixed comes precisely from that part of the spectrum band which both pigments have in common. But with our supposed monochromatic pigments, none of the characteristic curves would overlap. Consequently, any two of the pigments mixed would give black. Besides, the pigments themselves would probably have a very unpleasant color quality, like the crudity of red or green neon lights, which are crude because their light is largely made up of monochromatic emissions. Real monochromatic light, the light given off by a laser, looks as peculiar and unnatural to the eye as a pure electronic tone sounds to the ear.

Now that we have started constructing imaginary pigments, let us go on to construct a really useful set. As we have seen, a series of monochromatic pigments—each one reflecting nothing of the spectrum except in the narrow region of its own color name—would be of no use to paint with. But a set of exactly the opposite kind would be marvelous for painting; their mixtures would furnish all the brightest colors. Suppose that it were possible to find or to construct six pigments, each one reflecting all the visible spectrum *except* the particular region marked off by one of the color names. (Six, because the name "violet" does not correspond to a part of the spectrum. Let us take "indigo" to mean the blue-violet end.) Call these six pigments the minus colors. Thus, minus indigo would reflect all the blue, green, yellow, orange, and red of the spectrum. Minus blue would reflect the indigo, green, yellow, orange, and red, and so on. It is a little difficult to imagine what pigments like this would look like. They would probably be a range of luminous mauve and lavender grays without any decided color cast. But mixing the minus indigo with the minus blue would remove all the blue and indigo from the light they reflect, leaving only green, yellow, orange, and red, which would appear to the eye as a brilliant, clear, pale yellow. In the same way, mixing minus red and minus orange would produce a particularly brilliant blue-green. Minus green, minus yellow, and minus orange would give a luminous violet. Minus blue added to this mixture would give a rich purple. Adding minus indigo to this would give a dark red. The further addition of minus red would then give black.

All this sounds fantastic and impossible. Nevertheless, as the late Dr. Herbert Ives of the Bell Laboratories discovered, if one simplifies the system by limiting it to three minus colors, taking minus red, minus green, and minus blue as primaries, it turns out to be perfectly feasible and extremely useful. According to Dr. Ives,[*] monastral blue, which we have met before, reflects most of the blue and green of the spectrum and very little of the red, and thus can be taken as our minus red. Pale cadmium yellow reflects most of the red and green and very little of the blue, and so can serve as minus blue. The minus green is more difficult. There is no pigment or dye available today which reflects all the red and blue and none of the green. Dr. Ives nevertheless found that phospho-molybdo-tungstic acid lake of rhodamine 6G, a mauve-colored printers'-ink pigment, though not perfect, could be made to serve. Using these three colors alone with white, one can produce extraordinarily brilliant colors, particularly in the mauves, purples, blues, greens, and yellows. The rhodamine dye is not a perfect minus green, consequently, one cannot get very bright reds and oranges. However, if one fudges a little and uses a good cadmium red to fill out the gap, brighter pictures can be painted with these four pigments than with all the pigments the painter normally employs. Grays and degraded tones are a little difficult to make and manage; the basic pigments are all so strong that the slightest touch of one of them added to a gray to tone it is more likely to turn it

[*] Ives, "Thomas Young and the Simplification of the Artist's Palette." Proceedings of the Physical Society of London, Vol. 46 (January 1934), pp. 16–34.

from gray to a definite and even vivid color. On the other hand, the bright tones one paints are very bright indeed, and are apparently fairly permanent. At any rate, there are pictures of my own, painted more than twenty years ago with the four pigments, which are still amazingly vivid in color and show no sign of change.

As one can see from all this, color theory today is a complicated matter. And though something is beginning to be known about color as it occurs in nature, how color is perceived by the eye is still hardly understood at all. In fact, how little is known about the mechanism of color vision becomes very evident when one tries to account for a method of two-color photography which Dr. Edwin Land of the Polaroid Company recently came on to.[*] The process, as he describes it, uses two black-and-white photographs of a subject, taken one after the other through two different color filters. It makes very little difference, apparently, what color the filters are. They can be in any color range, can even be quite closely related hues. Dr. Land himself employed an orange yellow and a yellow green. The black-and-white negatives are printed as transparencies, put into separate projectors and projected superimposed on a screen, each through its own color filter. The resulting image is not as one would have anticipated, in tones of yellow. It looks like a quite ordinary color photograph with all the colors of the subject quite accurately reported. How two colors, apparently mono-chromatic and lying close together in the spectrum band, can serve to generate all of the colors from red to indigo, is difficult to explain.

I myself have had the good fortune to have had this effect demonstrated at the Bell Laboratories in Holmdel, New Jersey, by Mr. Charles R. Rubenstein and Mr. Donald E. Person, who are investigating its possible use in video tele-phone transmission. Their version employs a red and a green filter instead of two yellow ones for making the black-and-white slides. When the slides are projected together on the screen, the green filter is left off; using red and white light only seems to give more convincing color. The image obtained with this exhibits all the colors of nature except blue—bright reds, the brightest greens, good violets, mauves and oranges, and even a fairly clear yellow. Blue, when photographed by this method, comes out a slatey gray. If a good blue is needed, or a really good yellow, one must use three black-and-white slides, photographed through red, blue, and green filters and projected with respectively red, blue, and white lights.

More curious even than this and to me quite inexplicable: two gray-and-

[*] M. H. Wilson and R. W. Brocklebank, "Land's System of Two-color Projection." Bibl. British Institute Radio Engineering, J21 (June 1961), pp. 525–26.

white checkerboard plaids are made up of the same shape and size, but actually quite different because each square of the two plaids has been taken at random from a series of grays going by regular steps from black to white. The two checkerboards are then made into slides and projected together on a screen through two projectors, one fitted with a red filter and the other with no filter at all, just as above. If the tones of the squares have been picked at random—by a computer, or by throws of dice, or from a series of random numbers—the plaid projected on the screen will be in colors that can be named and graded—greens, oranges, mauves, and so on, some of them bright and some of them muted. But if the grays have been arranged on the checkerboards in a regular sequence, the eye is not fooled and will see only a series of reds and pinks. I, for one, do not know of any theory of vision which could account for such effects.

However this may be, we do know today that the color of a pigment, or of an object in nature, is never a pure spectrum hue, but is in reality a complicated chord of colors. This fact removes all pretense to scientific exactitude from the Munsell system of color classification; both the color circle and its extension, the color solid, are based on the notion that the hue factor of a color tone can be denoted by point position in the spectrum band, and this we now know is not true. We also know that the color-value sequence, on which Dr. Ross based his more difficult palettes, is largely an effect of chance. The color-value sequence— the idea that yellow is necessarily the palest of the bright colors and that violet is necessarily the darkest—turns out, like the eighteenth-century theory of primaries, to be in large part due to the accidental characteristics of the pigments we happen to have on hand. Yellow, of course, is naturally a pale color; the eye is more sensitive to yellow and yellow-green light than to red or blue. But we have been led to think of yellow as even paler than this because we have no pigment which reflects the yellow part of the spectrum only. When we think of yellow, we think quite naturally of our brightest yellow pigment, which is pale cadmium yellow. This, the brightest and palest of all yellow pigments, reflects, as I have pointed out, not only all the yellow of the spectrum but almost all the red and all the green as well, in fact, two whole thirds of the incident light, and consequently is a great deal paler and more luminous than a simple monochromatic yellow could possibly be. And as for violet, the painter naturally thinks of the violet which he has most commonly at hand and which he mixes from alizarin crimson and ultramarine blue. This mixture, like all mixtures of pigments, reflects considerably less light than either of its components would reflect alone, and on this account is a dark and heavy color. Pale cobalt violet, an opaque color,

---

151

expensive and little used, so poisonous, in fact, that its sale is forbidden in France, not being a mixture, reflects so much light in the red and blue regions that its value level is about that of vermillion. And baryte green, an intense, permanent but little known blue-green pigment, is so luminous that its value level is that of cadmium orange-yellow. Neither of these pigments will fit into the color-value sequence.

The color circle is suspect for another reason besides those connected with the notion of hue. The names of the colors on its rim should logically correspond to particular regions of the spectrum. But, as I have already pointed out, there is no spectrum region which corresponds to the name violet. The red and indigo ends of the spectrum have no point in common. Purple is not a color of the rainbow. It is the name we give to the sensation of seeing red and blue at the same time. Only symbolically—like the serpent of eternity which reassuringly bites its own tail—can the spectrum be bent back on itself to form a color circle.* Just the same, both the color circle and the color-value sequence have considerable practical justification, for though they will not serve to explain color as it occurs in nature, they nevertheless serve in a rough but useful fashion to explain how the pigments which we use behave (Fig. 41).

Forgetting that the term *hue* has no precise scientific meaning, let us treat the color circle as if it were a chart and mark it with a point to represent one of the painter's pigments, say a cobalt blue. Cobalt is a very bright blue, and the point representing it would lie very near the rim at B. Draw a line from this dot to the center of the circle, which in our chart stands for gray. Now all the degraded blues and blue grays which can be got by mixing cobalt with gray paint will fall along this line (Col. Fig. 8).

Now put down another dot to represent another pigment, say venetian red. This is a degraded color, and the point representing it would fall somewhere in the middle of a spoke running from the gray center to the point on the rim which stands for bright red orange. If then one draws a line from venetian red to

* Actually, the Munsell Color Circle is no longer used by physicists, largely for this very reason. It has been replaced by what is called the I.C.E. curve, a roughly horseshoe-shaped curve, each point of which represents a particular spectrum frequency. Since the curve is open— the red branch goes off in one direction and the blue in another—a straight line is drawn between red and indigo to represent arbitrarily the mauves and purples, which have no spectrum equivalents. The space enclosed between the curve and the line corresponds to the area of degraded tones lying within the color circle, with neutral gray somewhere in the middle of it (Fig. 41). The same objection, however, still applies to the I.C.E. curve as to the Munsell circle: The color of a pigment or of a tone in nature is much too complex to be represented by a point located in an area.

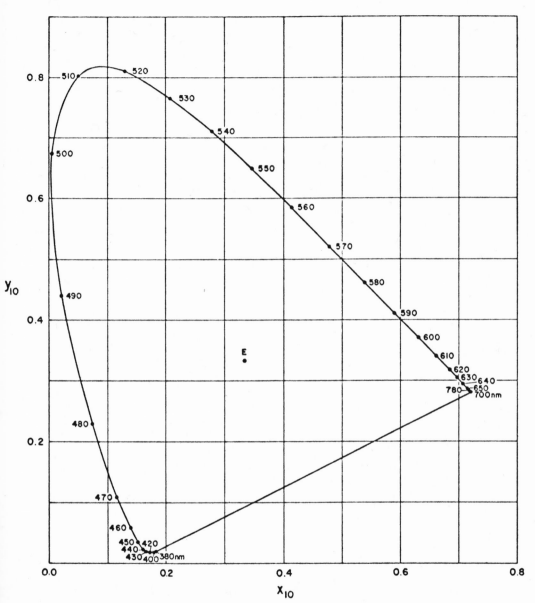

Fig. 41. I. C. E. Curve.

153

cobalt, all the tones to be got by mixing the two pigments will fall along it. This line will intersect the violet and red spokes of the diagram quite near the center. This indicates that a mixture of cobalt and venetian red can be made to give dull reds and violets. But since the line does not actually touch the center, a real neutral gray can not be made from these two pigments by themselves. For this, one needs another pigment. Yellow ocher will do. Put down a dot to represent this pigment half way along the yellow-orange spoke and draw lines from it to cobalt and venetian red. The triangle thus formed encloses the gray center—now we can mix gray—and any point within the triangle represents a tone that can be mixed from our three pigments (See Col. Fig. 8).

How will a green made with cadmium yellow and viridian differ from one made from cadmium yellow and cobalt blue? Set up the points on our diagram (Col. Fig. 9) and one sees at once that the line from cadmium yellow to viridian crosses the green spoke farther away from the center than the line drawn to cobalt blue. Hence viridian with cadmium yellow gives the brighter green.

Suppose, using the same center, one draws a smaller circle within the color circle (Col. Fig. 10). The small circle will then enclose all the tones needed for painting in a lowered key, where all the color relations are preserved but every color muted. This transposition, particularly effective in large pictures, was habitually used by the sixteenth- and seventeenth-century painters who removed all bright pigments from the palette and got their color contrasts by careful oppositions of warms and colds.

Now slip the smaller circle over till it touches the rim of the large circle at the yellow point (Col. Fig. 11). This will illustrate what takes place when one paints in a yellow tonality. The small circle contains all the tones one will be using in such a picture. Its center, the tone which will tell as gray in our picture, falls on a point of the large circle which stands for a degraded yellow; what will tell as a neutral gray in our picture is actually a tan. The twelve hues on the rim of the small circle have all kept their position in relation to one another, but their placement in the large circle shows that they have all been shifted toward yellow. The color we are using for red is actually a red-orange and our blue is a blue-green. The colors on the violet side are considerably dulled, and a dead gray-violet stands for purple. Nevertheless, all the color relations have been maintained. It is as if we were looking at the picture through a yellow glass.

This particular deformation of color was regularly practiced by the Renaissance painters to make their blues appear brighter and the orange red of their vermillion tell as scarlet. Think of Titian and Poussin, for example, with their extraordinarily luminous skies, almost phosphorescent in appearance because purposely placed out of key with the yellow tonality of the rest of the picture. The usual way of getting a yellow tonality is to work on a canvas washed with a tan or yellow tone, and to use viridian, which is a blue-green, in place of blue, and use for reds only the orange-red pigments like cadmium red-orange and venetian red. Since the cadmium reds and viridian keep their hue under incandescent electric light as cobalt and ultramarine and alizarin do not, this transposition is particularly useful for pictures which must be viewed at night. In this case, one must also eliminate the pale cadmium yellows, which by incandescent light become indistinguishable from white, and get one's yellows with yellow ocher and by mixing viridian with cadmium orange. A simpler way of arriving at a yellow tonality, of course, is to paint quite normally and then, when the picture is dry, to cover it all with a transparent yellow glaze. I myself have never found such glazes satisfactory. They take away from the freshness of the painting and give an old-master effect which seems rather distasteful today.

A similar displacement of color toward blue and green was invented and exhaustively explored by Spanish painters at the beginning of our century, as can be seen in the Museum of Modern Art in Madrid—pictures where a white tablecloth is actually bright blue, a face a purple-brown, and oranges in a dish a brown almost magenta. Picasso's early "blue period" is almost certainly inspired by them.

Such distortions can be very useful to the painter to help him arrive at unity of tone or color. The most usual way of going about it is the common practice, which I have mentioned above, of painting on a tinted ground. The tone of the ground automatically influences the painter's choice of color, and pushes the picture into that particular key. Rust-colored grounds, such as used by Goya, give warm pictures. Gray grounds produce cold ones. Boudin, I am convinced, kept on hand a series of canvases already prepared in tones of blues and gray, and chose for his picture a canvas whose ground color could be used as a base tone for the sky or weather he was about to paint. Léonid (Fig. 42), at one time or another, has used a somewhat similar system, one which could not be simpler or more effective. It consisted of mixing up a fairly large quantity of pale-gray paint—white with a little black and a touch of ocher or sienna added to kill the lilac tinge which black takes on when mixed with only white. Part of this paint is spread on the canvas and left to dry to furnish a ground tone for the picture. Part of it is put up in tubes to be used, exactly as if it were white, for mixing up tones when painting. The real white paint takes its place on the palette along with the other colors, to be used for accents or for mixing up tones needing to be lighter than the basic gray. In this way, all the pale passages of the picture, the sky, the distant planes, the highlights of the foreground, passages which are done with very little pure color and much gray paint, are automatically grayed and softened and brought down in value, while the deeper tones, in landscape chiefly to be found in the nearer objects, have little of the gray in them and keep their normal value level and normal intensity of color. Thus, the picture acquires a unity of tonality without the bright colors being unduly degraded. And since the gray paint with which the tones are all mixed is the exact color of the painting ground itself, it becomes very easy to make distant objects merge into the sky and to produce those effects of misty air and milky light for which Léonid himself is so well known (Fig. 42A).

The color-value sequence can also be used as a framework for color transpositions, and can serve to explain how the virtuoso painters of the nineteenth century such as Manet, Zorn, Chase, Sargent, or Sorolla managed to heighten their color without ever departing from the conventions of naturalism. These painters transcribed the tones of nature as they saw them, keeping each tone at its proper hue and value; that is to say, a blue in nature came out in the picture as a blue, a light as a light tone, a dark as a dark tone. The color intensity of the tones, on the other hand, they systematically heightened. The brighter tones of their subject, those which were highly colored in nature, they painted as they found them. But the duller tones they arbitrarily brought up to higher intensity, sometimes, for particularly brilliant effects, to the highest intensity possible at that particular value level. For example, a dead brown in the subject would be transcribed as a burnt orange and a pale gray as a bright lavender or blue, changes which were not enough to appear unnatural or inconsistent, but which were very useful in making the color sing.

The color-value sequence has an even more important place in the color system used by the Fauves and the German Expressionists. These painters carefully conserved the dark-and-light values and the contrasts of warms and colds which they found in the subjects they were painting. The hues, however, they conventionalized. Each tone in nature was arbitrarily heightened to the brightest color occurring at its particular value level, the blue-green side of the color sequence being used for the cold tones and the orange-red side for the warm ones. Thus, all highlights were painted as bright yellow; middle tones

Fig. 42. LÉONID, Storm over Leyden, 1966. *Courtesy Larcada Gallery.*

Fig. 42A. LÉONID, Venice, IV, 1970. Oil on canvas. *Courtesy Larcada Gallery.*

became either red or green; darker tones were transcribed as mauve or blue, and all dark shadows as violet.

Generalizations such as these are useful to the painter because they offer him some valuable hints for going about his business. Their value is quite independent of the correctness of the theory behind them. And no color theory, however correct, can be made to furnish rules for turning out good color, even for good flat, decorative color. The only guide to color is to use it, to work with paints until one has learned to distinguish subtleties and relations visible only to an educated eye and until the painter can find instantly on the end of his brush the exact tone he has in mind, without ever stopping to think how it was done. This takes time and practice. No matter how good a sense of color the young painter is endowed with, its accurate expression is one of the last skills he acquires.

· 10 ·

PORTRAITS

AND PASTELS

LET US RETURN from this long technical discussion.

When World War II began, I was again in Paris, had come back in 1937, and was painting still lifes with the paints I had learned to make in America. I had a bicycle, a small pink studio from whose window I could look down into the courtyard of the *Ecole des Beaux-Arts,* and with this, very little money. But this did not bother me because a French picture dealer was beginning to take an interest in my work and my pictures were beginning to sell. However, I was finding the false calm of these early months of the war oppressive and was not tempted to sit them out in Paris, as some of my friends had decided to do. And when Julien Levy offered me a show in his New York gallery, I accepted. The only way to get the pictures to him was to bring them, and at the end of October I sailed from Bordeaux on what turned out to be the last transatlantic boat to leave from a French port. My New York show was reasonably successful, and when it was over, I went to stay with my mother and father, who were then living in Chattanooga—*le Château Nougat,* as the composer Henri Sauguet called it.

There I went to work to make myself at home. I got rid of the bicycle which I had brought with me—it was too strenuous for that hilly and motorized town—and acquired a motorcycle in its place. I found friends among the local artists and motorcycle riders, discovered a new subject for pictures in the decaying houses of the Negro section, and started looking for a way to make a little money painting.

The only possible way seemed to lie in portraits, for it was inconceivable that anyone at that time and in that part of the country would think of buying a picture with any other subject. Not that there was any lack of interest in painting itself. An active group of young painters, led by Frank Baisden, who ran the art department of the University of Chattanooga, put on frequent exhibitions of their work at the university library which were well attended and much appreciated. But none of the pictures were ever actually sold. The greatest remuneration an exhibitor could expect was a twenty-dollar prize and a mention in the papers. Today's current fashion for collecting painting had not yet come into existence. Today, even in the smallest town, any pretention to serious culture must be substantiated by a collection of original works by the available painters. But in the thirties, the most sumptuously decorated houses had only color prints, usually anonymous, generally of flowers, and always much more elaborately framed than they deserved, while an intellectual household would be distinguished by a varnished reproduction of Van Gogh's *Sunflowers.* There was indeed so little market for real pictures that during the six or seven years I spent in Chattanooga, despite the fact that I was the best-known painter there and highly respected on account of my out-of-town reputation, only one picture of mine was locally bought which was not a commissioned portrait. Portraiture was the only branch of painting for which there was the slightest demand. But this was a branch I was reluctant to cultivate. Clients for portraits are much too difficult to manage.

It is not just anybody who orders a portrait. In fact, sitters who are willing to pay money to endure the tedium of posing are a very special group which can be classified under a small number of headings. There are Club Presidents (or Royalty), Ancestors, Debutants (which include a subgroup of Sons in College), Young Matrons, and Children. And which of these categories one has to deal with determines how much trouble the picture will be to do.

A commissioned portrait, to be acceptable to a client, does not have to be an outstanding work of art. But there is one indispensable quality it must possess: The image of the sitter it presents must please the client and the client's family and friends. When the sitter is a simple debutant or college student, this is not too difficult to achieve. Even the least prepossessing of them will have a certain freshness and the charm of youth. All the painter has to do is make them sit still and paint them as they are. The same applies to children, with however this exasperating qualification, that a child cannot by any means or artifice be made to sit still at all. The club president, again offers no difficulty. By his very position he will be a man of character, even of distinction. The painter has only to underline this distinction and everybody is satisfied. Unfortunately for a newcomer to the field such as I was, portraits of chief justices and college presidents are usually turned over to painters who have already gained a reputation for chief justices and college presidents, and not to any casual untried local man. The few such sitters that might come his way, however, will be easy to paint and not at all hard to please. Young matrons and ancestors, on the other hand, present great difficulty. The young matron will certainly have put off ordering her portrait until she has perceived that her beauty has begun to fade. The portrait is being commissioned for two reasons: to preserve an image of her beauty for her husband and for her children, and to reassure the sitter herself. Thus the painter is expected to pull up a sagging jawline, smooth out wrinkles, revivify a tired skin, and paint the sitter as she was some years before. In much the same way, a painter dealing with the very old cannot paint them frankly as he sees them. He is hired to create an ancestor figure intended to enhance the prestige of the client's family, and the illness and degeneration he cannot help but see in his sitter would be both distressing and irrelevant in such an image. He must paint the sitters as they appeared a decade earlier so that they can be remembered as still vigorous and impressive. A painter I know was offered a particularly troublesome commission of this sort—a double portrait of a husband and wife, the wife very old and the husband dead, the husband to be done from a photograph taken some thirty years before, and the wife to be painted from life, but suitably rejuvenated to match the photograph. I cannot imagine that the picture turned out well.

From the client's point of view, such desires seem quite legitimate. To the painter, they are absurd and degrading strictures. What he particularly resents is that he is being asked to exercise an extrasensory talent which he undoubtedly possesses but which he cannot call to his aid by act of will. He is asked to see through his clients' eyes and to reconstruct on canvas something that the clients themselves can only vaguely remember. His work is bound to become tentative, for he cannot be sure that what he is putting down is right, nor can his clients be sure either. The sittings drag on interminably, the picture never seems to get done, and when it is finished, no matter how pleased the clients may be, the painter hates it.

Portraits of children, on the other hand, can never drag. Painting a child offers the disconcerting advantage that by the end of the fourth or fifth sitting the picture has to be finished. No matter how friendly and well-disposed the child may be, his nervous system will not accept more than this. During the first sitting, the child will probably be quiet enough and reasonably attentive. In the second, the painter will need all his charm to get his model back into his seat. During the third, it will take a display of temper and the nurse's help to even keep him in the room. As for the fourth and fifth sittings, the painter will pass them alone, without a sitter, working from memory. Under such circumstances, detailed and studied painting is hardly possible. But a likeness that will please is not too difficult to get. All children are fresh and pretty. They grow and change so rapidly that the parents seldom have an exact idea of what they look like. The children themselves could not care less. And any reasonably convincing image of something that is not a monster will be enthusiastically accepted by everybody. Portraits of children, I should imagine, are commissioned not so much to show the child off, or to record what he looked like, but rather to prove to the child himself that he is loved, for I have noticed that most of the children I have been asked to paint had been adopted. However this may be, whether children in America are particularly pampered, or whether children, like flowers, are considered particularly suitable subjects for cheerful and decorative pictures, requests for children's portraits far outnumber all the other commissions a painter in the provinces is offered. Moreover, in a large provincial town like Chattanooga, where all the well-to-do parents know one another and all their children go to the same schools, a successful portrait of one child always engenders others. In a large capital, like Chicago or New York, this will not be true. Here the field is too large and too diversified. Parents are linked together by social and business interests and not by the bonds of a school which their children happen to attend. And it takes a great deal more than one or two successful portraits to establish a painter's reputation or create a clientele.

In view of all this, if I was doomed to paint portraits, portraits of children seemed the most promising, easiest to come by, hard on the nerves and patience, perhaps, but quickest finished and done with. A decorator friend of my mother's suggested pastel, which she said, voicing a common opinion, was so pretty for children. Pastel had also the serious advantage of being less imposing than oil, actually only a sort of colored drawing which, as a drawing, could be offered at lower prices than my New York gallery was asking for my oils; low prices can be very useful when one is trying to break into a new market. I had no experience whatever with pastel; I think I had never held a stick of it in my hand. But I looked pastels up in a book, got out my pigment powders, and made a set which seemed to work quite well. With this, I did heads of the decorator's two children and gave them to her to use as samples. Out of this came a couple of commissions, and then some more, till eventually I had done almost all the children in the leading private school. My reputation was entirely local. I tried in every way to spread it to the neighboring Atlanta but with no success whatever, nor could I bring it to New York. I believe I was regarded not as an artist but as an independent journeyman, for I would arrive at the client's house on a motorcycle with my painting kit strapped on like a set of tools, try to keep out of the parents' way as much as possible, and to reserve my best graces for the servants who could help me keep the children still. Eventually, I had a small accident with the motorcycle and gave it up to buy a car. That, and also perhaps my prices, which had gone up, spoiled my status as an honest workman, for the number of my commissions dropped, and I began to receive invitations to dinner instead. But by this time I had grown very tired of painting children and glad to have an excuse to give it up.

I had made up my own pastels when I began doing children because I did not trust the manufactured colors. There were beautiful and tempting sets at the local artists'-supply shop, but I had no way of finding out what pigments went into them, and I preferred to use only those pigments I had been told were stable. Besides, pastels are quite easy to make. They are only sticks of powdered pigment held together by some weak binder. The painter, Arthur Dove, who also made his own pastels, used a dilute solution of gum tragacanth in water. I myself settled for water in which a little oatmeal had been boiled. The binder must be very weak. It does not function to bind the pigment particles to the paper, only to keep the sticks themselves from crumbling. And if it is too strong, the sticks dry out too hard and cannot be made to write.

Each pigment one is intending to use in the set must be made up into a series of sticks grading in tone from pure pigment to a tinted white. One begins by putting out two small piles of dry pigment on the grinding slab, one of white and the other, say, of cobalt blue, wets them with the binding liquid, and works them with the knife to the consistency of stiff clay. The blue pile is then divided in half. One half is put on a piece of waxed paper and rolled, exactly as one would roll a cigarette, to make a cylinder the size of a cigarette but somewhat thicker. This, when dry, will be the darkest stick of this particular series. For the next darkest stick, the leftover half of cobalt paste is mixed with an equal bulk of the white paste, the mixture is again divided into halves, one half rolled into a stick, the other half mixed with an equal quantity of white, and so on. The process is repeated until eight or ten sticks have been made, each stick paler than the one before it. The final stick will be almost indistinguishable from white.

When the sticks are thoroughly dry, they must be tried out on paper to see if they are soft enough to write properly. If a stick is too hard, it can be mashed into a paste with plain water, formed again into a stick, and left to dry, when it should come out softer. If, on the contrary, the sticks dry out too soft and crumbly, they can be crushed and remade with stronger oatmeal water.

Arthur Dove had an even simpler way of forming pastel sticks. He mixed the powdered pigments with enough of his gum tragacanth solution to make a thin, almost soupy mud. Then, using a palette knife as if it were a trowel, he would slap down a bladeful of the mud on a piece of paper and leave it there to dry. No attempt was made to round it into a cylinder; the points and thin edges of the stick are very useful for drawing lines. Dove's sticks were more porous in texture than my rolled ones, quicker to break and crumble. My slightly tougher oatmeal-water sticks were probably better for the sort of drawings in color which my pastel portraits turned out to be. But if one is using pastels like paint, in broad areas and carefully related tones and values, then Arthur Dove's sort of pastels are far superior.

In addition to the usual pastel series compounded of a pigment and white, Dove would also prepare a series of dark tones made from the same pigment and black. Such dark tones are marvelously rich and cannot be found in the commercial sets. One needs only the three or four upper tones of a series. The darker tones are indistinguishable from black and consequently superfluous. In the same way, the very pale tones of some of the pigments can be omitted. The pale tones of cadmium red and venetian red, for example, cannot be told apart, nor can the pale tones of alizarin and indian red.

Ivory black and lamp black do not make up into satisfactory sticks. The pigments are greasy and difficult to wet. Mars black or some other mineral black should be used instead. The dark tones of monastral blue and of alizarin crimson, pigments which have little body and great tinting strength, become so hard in drying that they will not make a mark on paper. This also happens with some of the earth colors, which behave like clay and dry brick-hard. A little soap added to the binder is said to remedy this. It does not always work.

Pastel has a peculiarity that sets it apart from all the other ways of painting: color mixtures in pastel are predominantly additive. When a stick of yellow and a stick of blue are put on together, the two tones lie on the paper as separate specks of color and behave, on a smaller scale, like the dots of color used in Impressionist technique. Subtractive mixing, such as one gets with paints, plays a much smaller part. So that in pastel, mixing a yellow and a blue gives something which is nearer gray than green. Consequently, pastel is poor in greens compared to oil or watercolor. If one is going to need a variety of bright greens or yellow greens in a picture, each of the hues must be made up as a separate series, by first mixing the deep tone out of the appropriate pigments and then making it into a series with white. For the same reason, because the mixtures are largely additive, pastel is surprisingly rich in mauves and reds. Sticks of cadmium red and alizarin put on together give tones of red impossible to achieve in oil.

The traditional white for making pastels is whiting or powdered chalk. In fact, pastel is only a fancier name for colored chalks. Whiting is solid and chemically inert but not very opaque. Lithopone and zinc white, which are more opaque, are also used. I thought to make pastels with particularly great covering power by using titanium white instead, which is the most opaque of all white pigments. Titanium-based pastels are very dense. They have as well a certain waxy quality which makes them stick to the paper, and a great deal more correcting and changing is possible with them than with pastels made of chalk. I must confess, however, that I was so pleased with my titanium pastels that I never got around to making any of the chalk- or the zinc-based ones, so I have no real idea how the three sorts compare.

Pastels are done on paper. In large works, like the seventeenth-century copy of a Veronese done in pastel which hangs in the Naples Museum, the paper is usually mounted on canvas. There are various sorts of pastel papers. All of them are tinted. Some of them have a sandpaper or a velourlike surface which accepts more pigment from the sticks than plain paper will and gives a richer effect. But these special surfaces are easily marred by overworking, and a spot where the texture has been worn away can never be satisfactorily mended. I myself used ordinary charcoal paper, which comes in all sorts of agreeable tints of gray and tan and pink, and which can be found anywhere. The local frame-maker would mount the paper on cardboard for me, pasting a sheet on both sides of the board to equalize the pull of the paste as it dried and keep the board from warping. For outlines and accents, I used black Conté crayon, which comes in various degrees of hardness and can be sharpened to a point. The great covering power of the titanium-based pastels made things fairly easy to correct and change without too much erasing. For erasing one used the same kneaded rubber used in charcoal drawing. If a large area had to be changed, or if a particular spot became slicked down from overworking, the pastel dust could be cleaned off, the surface of the paper refreshed, and its tooth restored by going over it with sandpaper.

The greatest inconvenience of pastels, when working with them, lies in the difficulty of getting ones hands on the particular stick one needs. All the sticks get quickly broken and indistinguishably concealed under an identical gray dust which coats them all. To discover the color of a piece, one has to make a mark with it, an interminable process of trial and error. If the different hues could only be kept apart, one would save both time and effort. But inescapably, in the heat of working, the sticks get shuffled around like dominos, the pieces broken into smaller pieces, too small either to find or to use. However, when the confusion becomes unendurable, there is a perfect if drastic remedy. The fragments can be matched and reassembled, crushed up with water, reformed into sticks, and the set returned to its all too transitory order. And if a set of pastels is periodically thus refreshed, it will last indefinitely.

Despite its evident fragility, pastel is a fairly safe and permanent way of working. It has no binding medium, no oil or glue or varnish, to yellow or crack or spoil. And if the paper is protected from dust and damp, if the pigments used are inert and lightproof, and if the picture is not hung in direct sunlight, which will fade even the reputedly lightproof pigments, there is no reason why a pastel should ever change. Except that the pigments hold to the paper only by being caught in the grain, and the slightest touch will smear them. There are various fixitives for pastel, solutions of gelatine, or gums and varnishes in volatile solvents, which can be sprayed on to bind the pigment particles in place. But not one of them will leave the pastel as it was. When a pastel is fixed, the light tones invariably sink and all the colors change and darken. This is why:

The mark a pastel makes on paper, looked at through a microscope, is a loose heap of particles which acts as a light trap. A ray of light entering the heap bounces from particle to particle to emerge with more saturated color than if it had only encountered one colored surface. Pastel, in fact, behaves like velvet, which always appears richer in color than the thread it is woven from because of the multiple reflections of light caught in the maze of upright threads. But, when pastel is sprayed with a fixitive, the loose heap of particles collapses, the surface tension of the liquid pulls it down, and it no longer acts as a light trap. In addition to this, the particles themselves, now coated with gum or varnish, lose much of their opacity, and the color mixtures, which before were additive, become subtractive, so that everything turns darker and heavier and the values and colors are all thrown out of balance.

Degas, just the same, apparently had some sort of pastel fixitive which he used. At any rate, none of his pastels seems to have suffered excessively from wear or rubbing. Certainly they are quite valuable enough to have always been very carefully protected. But I am told that he probably employed a weak solution of dammar in acetone sprayed on twice during the work—once after the placement and color of everything had been established, and then onto the finished work, which was thereupon gone over again with fresh pastel to correct all the changes in tone which the second coat of fixitive had caused. But even elaborate fixing such as this serves only to keep the pigment particles from dusting off the paper by their own weight. It will not protect the pastel from serious smearing or rubbing.

My own pastels I did not attempt to fix. I would do nothing but have them immediately framed, put under glass with a thick mat of cardboard to prevent the glass from touching the paper, and with the edges sealed with tape to keep out air and dust. They had been done as commissions, to be framed and delivered as soon as finished, and did not have to risk the dangers they would have incurred lying unframed around a studio. Unframed pastels are much too fragile to store in a portfolio, and framing everything one does is a great nuisance and a great expense. Consequently, I have never used pastel for work other than these portraits. This I regret, for of all the ways of painting, pastel provides the most beautiful color quality and is the simplest and fastest to work with.

I regret even more that I was led to spend so long a time at what is really a nonprofessional activity. By nonprofessional activity, I mean work in a professional field done in obedience to some extraprofessional directive—such as doctors being put to work at biological warfare or poets at advertising. A nonprofessional activity is what portrait painting has now become. And I do not believe that a painter can engage in it for long without getting hurt. Certainly, the several years I worked at portraiture took away all my interest in painting portraits along with my ability to do disinterested ones.

The peculiar characteristic of portraiture is that a portrait must achieve two separate aims which have little in common. A portrait must first be professionally acceptable. This is to say that its composition should balance, its color be harmonious, and it should be competently drawn and painted. Also, and quite apart from this, it must present a convincing likeness of the sitter, which indeed is the reason it has been ordered. These two aims require quite different talents. A portrait can be superbly drawn and painted and still look nothing like the sitter, while a work, which from a professional point of view has nothing to excuse it, presents a speaking likeness. If the problem were only that of turning out a well-painted head or figure, the painter would need nothing more than the same skill and talent that have gone to make his other works professionally acceptable. But to produce a convincing representation of the sitter requires something quite different. For this, the painter must have the ability to stand apart from the sitter, to look at him coolly and objectively, even, if necessary, ruthlessly, and to select, underline and even exaggerate those traits and attitudes and those particular forms and proportions of face and body which convey the clearest image of the sitter's character. The painter does not need the greatest gifts for painting. He needs only an acute eye, considerable detachment, and an intuition not unmixed with malice—in short, a gift for caricature.

But above all, he needs the kind of sitter who can accept so cool a representation, a sitter sure of himself and his position in the world, and not requiring extra reassurance from the painter. In any good portrait from any period, from the bronze and marble Roman heads by Hellenistic sculptors to Picasso's portrait of Gertrude Stein, the artist has been permitted to look at his sitter from the outside and describe him in objective and not necessarily flattering terms. Charles V's Hapsburg lip, which Titian faithfully rendered, is brutally ugly. And it is difficult for us today to understand how a simple burgher, such as Titian was, could have dared to affront so powerful a prince. We forget that the Hapsburg lip was to its bearer not a deformity but the mark of the bluest blood in Christendom, which the painter was expected to point up, not to suppress. In all such portraits, what the sitter demanded of the painter was the exterior marks of caste and character, the traits which would describe the sitter's rank, race, wealth, intelligence, distinction, and so on. To this list of desirable qualities, the eighteenth-century sitters added first condescension, then affability, and finally charm. Charm, however, is a great deal more difficult for a painter to deal with than the others, for charm is not a quality which lends itself to caricature. It is actually the expression of the way the sitter sees himself, and consequently, it can be approached and apprehended only by a sort of spiritual communion of painter and sitter. Even the most repellent characters are charming if looked at from the point of view they take to see themselves. Thus, to render a sitter's charm, the painter must exercise an extrasensory talent and get inside him. What is required of the painter is not really flattery. He is asked to do only what the sitter is accustomed to do for himself—to understand and to forgive. The sort of extralucid state of mind necessary for such interior communion is tricky to establish and exhausting to maintain. And once it is established, unless the painter is very tough indeed, he will become dominated by the sitter, he will forgive too much, and the portrait will come out lacking in character. It is in no way surprising that the work of the eighteenth-century portraitists who delt in charm, such as Gainsborough, La Tour, or Mme Vigée-Lebrun, is consistently less direct, less manly, and less successful than that of the painters like Titian, El Greco, or Terborch who preceded them.

Today, it is even harder for a painter to turn out an objective, impersonal portrait. Today's sitter does not particularly wish to impose. In fact, he is rather afraid of appearing too distinguished. Nor does he really consider it necessary for the portrait to present a particularly striking likeness; he is convinced that a camera will always give a better one. He requires only that the portrait show him as charming and seductive. The painter is not called on to see and to record; he is asked to reassure. He must step down from his detachment as recording angel to become a yes-man, to relinquish vision for sympathy, and the objective description of character for a vague and generalized eulogy—in sum, to perform a nonprofessional service.

Under any conditions, the creation of a likeness is an obscure and very mysterious process. And I, for one, do not at all understand how it works or how the likeness is obtained. A spot of color or an accent, which do not help the color or drawing in any way, will suddenly cause the likeness to become alive, while a stroke that advances the drawing immensely will completely obliterate the likeness. During the course of painting, the likeness comes and goes, appears and vanishes as unaccountably as clouds before the moon. A great deal depends on the state of fatigue of the sitter and whether or not he feels at ease with the painter, who quickly learns to coddle and pamper his sitter out of all measure. In such a process, the likeness, its presence or absence, takes on overwhelming importance. And since a likeness is what the client is buying, once the likeness is established, it becomes difficult for the painter to go on with the work, no matter how unorganized or unfinished the rest of the picture may be.

The principal reason for our great trouble with portraiture today, I suspect, is that the painter no longer has backing from his profession, such as the guilds once provided, which would give him support to face his client, and it has become difficult for him to be properly tough. In the state of sympathy he has had to establish for the painting, the sitter's faults and weaknesses stand out so painfully clear to him that it seems both indiscreet and unnecessarily cruel to underline them. The painter forgets that the sitter has so often forgiven his mirror that he will not hesitate to forgive his portrait as well, however damnatory the painter himself may find it. So, fearing to shock and hesitating to displease, the painter attenuates the cruel traits, and the portrait comes out weak.

This is largely the reason for the bad name the professional portrait bears today and why the term "portrait painter" has acquired the same opprobrious overtones as "academic." Besides, the habits acquired in portrait painting are very hard to change. Once the painter has become broken to portrait painting, he will treat even his paid models as if they were portrait sitters, be oversensitive to their moods and painfully aware of their first twinge of boredom. He will look for a likeness that will charm the sitter, and once the likeness is found, will let the painting go. This is not the way proper painting is done. Here, as in every other sort of painting, the painter must dominate and control all the circumstances of the work and seek to please no one but himself and his professional conscience.

Consequently, whatever is good in portrait painting today is based on an honest cruelty. Sometimes the cruelty can be ignored by the sitter because it is used to endow him with a worldly elegance, as in the pictures of Van Dongen (Fig. 43), or in the terrifying series of Café Society figures done by the late René Bouché (Fig. 44). Sometimes the cruelty is so perceptive and biting that it becomes unacceptable even to the sitters themselves, as must certainly be the case with Alice Neel's portraits of Greenwich Village characters and New York intellectuals (Fig. 45). But unless the painter is ruthless and at heart a moralist, the portraits he turns out, no matter how skillfully painted, will belong to commercial art.

Unfortunately there is very little demand today for any of this. Likeness by photography is so easy, current, inexpensive, and convincing. And a formal portrait in the drawing room provides a less imposing status symbol than any current abstraction by a known name, besides being much less easy to fit into a contemporary-style interior.

Fig. 43. VAN DONGEN, Modjesko, Soprano Singer, 1908. Collection, The Museum of Modern Art. Gift of Mr. and Mrs. Peter A. Rübel.

Fig. 44. RENÉ BOUCHÉ, Mme. Hervé Alphand. *Courtesy Mrs. René Bouché.*

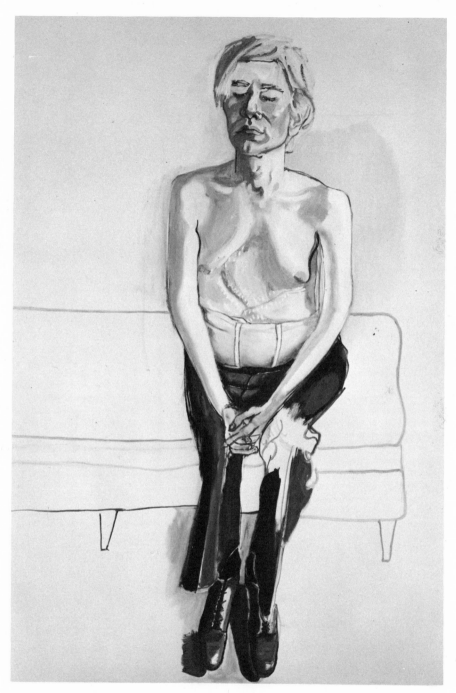

Fig. 45. ALICE NEEL, Andy Warhol, 1970. *Collection Whitney Museum.*

175

· 11 ·

LANDSCAPE

THE COUNTRY AROUND Chattanooga is gentle and beautiful, with a broad river, low mountains, and plains. Now that I had a motorcycle and was mobile, all this was at hand and waiting to be painted. But I did not know how to go about it. I had no idea what sort of landscape would make up into a picture or how to fit it onto canvas, nor had I any technique capable of handling it. The only landscapes I had ever painted were some student watercolors I had done at Harvard in the then current academic Impressionist manner, with washes of color over a pencil sketch, a limited technique especially suited to rendering the effects of bright sunlight out-of-doors. But this way of painting had by now been overworked to banality and besides was not at all appropriate to the country here.

A completely new subject, such as landscape was to me, is not easy for a painter to get into: It demands new ways of seeing and of painting which are quite outside his habits. And forbidding and inaccessible it will remain until he

177

contrives to discover in it some familiar element which will serve to tie it in with the things he already knows. Thus, with landscape painting, I saw no way of getting into it, until late one night I happened to wander through the Negro section of the town and there stumbled on the magic bridge I needed. And I suddenly realized that these smoke-stained houses with their peeling paint (Fig. 46), lined up under the harsh, infrequent street lights like people waiting for a parade to come were exactly what I had been painting all along. They were not only like objects set up for a still life; they were also sitters posing for a portrait. And the familiar means I already had at hand were quite enough for doing them. I had only to treat them as I would a still life, grouping the houses to fill my canvas, trying quite objectively to get their edges and colors and textures right, and at the same time trying, as in a portrait, to express their individual characters by underlining the almost human traits they had acquired by use and age. The results, if not exactly landscapes, would nevertheless serve as a path to get me there.

I thought I had best begin with the simplest possible version of the subject—like a still life of a single apple or a portrait with nothing but the sitter's head—and decided to paint pictures each containing one house only. I explored all the Negro sections of the town and made quick sketches of everything that looked promising. These I classed into morning and afternoon subjects and into subjects for bright days and for cloudy ones, so that I might have something to work on at all times of day and for most kinds of weather. I constructed a sort of view-finder out of two small right angles of cardboard marked off in quarter inches, which I used to frame and isolate the subject, find out how much of it I needed in the picture, and what shape and size canvas it would take. American canvas sizes are not standardized as they are in France; stretcher bars come in multiples of inches, in any length from eight inches up, which can be put together as one pleases. Thus, for each of the subjects I planned to paint, I would prepare a canvas whose proportions would leave little room for street or sky or other background, exactly as in a still life. And then I would set up my easel squarely in front of the house I had decided on and begin to paint, first in tempera and then going on in oil as I was in the habit of doing, giving particular attention to the house's peculiarities, just as if I were painting its portrait.

The sharp characterization which naturally resulted gave these first Chattanooga pictures of mine a deceptively Leftist air as if they had been intended as social comment, which was certainly not the case. They could scarcely have been called landscapes, not even urban landscapes. They were in reality only still lifes

Fig. 46. MAURICE GROSSER, Woodpile, 1946. *Artist's Collection.*

painted out-of-doors, in which the objects were things made of brick and stone and wood. But the houses themselves were so different one from another that, despite the limited formula I had adopted, the pictures came out varied and interesting enough to make up a second show at Julien Levy's gallery. Whereupon —as always happens when a group of recent work is shown, and the painter, by seeing them all together before the public, is able to find out what part of it comes off and what does not—my strict formula began to expand. In my next batch of pictures, the sky, fields, trees, and so on began to take on more importance, while the houses shrank to become a secondary element often not even needed. Until suddenly one day I discovered that my stratagem had worked, that I had all of the problems well in hand, and that I was beginning to paint legitimate open landscapes (Fig. 47).

Open landscape, landscape with vistas and distance, is quite different in its basic structure from any other sort of picture. The essential geometry of a still life or of a figure piece can be described as a set of bumps or, to put it more politely, as a group of objects protruding from a less important background. Whereas the basic geometrical pattern of an open landscape is a hole. And, for the painter, a hole is always more difficult to deal with than a projection, because, in a picture whose structure is based on a recession, the compositional elements are much more difficult to pull into balance.

From the point of view of composition, the strongest lines in any picture are the four sides of the canvas. Nothing inside a picture makes as heavy accents or strikes the eye as forcibly as the four lines where the picture ends. And a painter always takes great care to direct the spectator's eye away from them. He endeavors to put all principal forms and heavy accents well inside the central areas, and never places a strong accent or an abrupt change of value near the sides of a canvas or allows an important line to lead out of the picture by cutting into the frame.

In a still life or figure piece, this is all fairly easy. Here, the subject of the picture is made up of a limited number of objects—ten apples in a bowl, a mother and child, a head and shoulders—along with whatever background the objects have behind them. With such a concise subject, it is a relatively simple matter to group the objects on the canvas, to decide how much of the background is to be included, and to determine where the edges of the picture should fall for best effect. Important forms and strong accents find their place quite naturally in the central areas. And the accents and masses which come unavoidably near the frame can easily be attenuated and "thrown away" by reducing their value con-

Fig. 47. MAURICE GROSSER, Open Landscape, 1970. *Artist's Collection.*

trasts, by fuzzing their edges, or even by leaving their drawing a little vague.

In landscape all this is more difficult. Suppose we have an open landscape subject such as Claude or Turner would have painted (Fig. 48), with its three planes of distance—foreground, middle ground, and distant prospect. It presents itself to us as a large emptiness studded with innumerable objects. There is no fixed point at which the subject necessarily ends, and it is hard to decide how much of the view our picture should take in, what to include and what would weaken the picture if included. When this has been settled and the various elements, the trees, fields, mountains, and so on, have been assigned to their proper places, there still remains the problem presented by the strong accents in the foreground. The foreground, which necessarily occupies the bottom parts of the canvas, will have the heaviest accents and the strongest contrasts of lights and shadows. The top part of the canvas holds the sky and distant objects, which are considerably weaker in accents and contrasts. So that the bottom part of the canvas will be strong and heavy and the top will be light and weak and one will have to exert considerable ingenuity to coax the two disparate halves to balance.

For the same reason—strong accents which lie unavoidably near the edges of the canvas—a landscape framed in trees, or glimpsed through an archway, no matter how attractive the subject may appear in nature, can never be made up into a satisfactory picture. The subject itself, the mountain or the sunset, is greatly enhanced by being framed and isolated, just as a picture is. But when the frame of foliage or masonry is itself put on canvas, its dark values and strong accents give such weight to the edges of the picture that the enclosed landscape motif, which has no such accents, is reduced to nullity.

In an open landscape, the foreground details have usually not much pictorial importance. They serve rather to lead up to, and to situate, the objects in the far and middle distance which constitute the real center of interest. And one of the great differences between landscape and all other sorts of painting lies in the treatment which must be given these distant objects. The landscape painter, unlike the still life or figure painter, is not at all concerned in exhibiting their solid masses. His chief concern is to show how far they are away. There are various devices for this. Occasionally, even strict geometrical perspective will serve if the subject contains convenient rows of objects, like fence posts, which grow smaller as they lead into the distance, or parallel lines, which draw together to a vanishing point. A geometrical vanishing point, however, makes so strong an accent in a picture that it can be difficult to manage. Much more useful is the device of showing one object to be nearer than another by making it hide

Fig. 48. TURNER, East Cowes Castle, Isle of Wight, 1828. Oil on canvas.
Courtesy Victoria & Albert Museum, London.

part of the one behind, or by drawing very clearly the retreating surface of land or field on which both objects lie. More useful than any of this, in fact the one indispensable tool for demonstrating space and distance, is aerial perspective, a device which I have already described at length and which, besides, can be found expounded in complete detail in Leonardo's notebooks. This is how it works:

Between the painter and the landscape he is painting hangs a curtain of air, transparent but by no means invisible. This intervening air, which hardly enters at all into still life or figure painting, is the landscape painter's prime consideration. For him, air and distance are almost interchangeable terms; the one can scarcely be painted without the other. In fact, the layer of air between him and the horizon is the principal object in his picture, and the sky which he must paint is itself nothing but a mass of air put on show against the black of interstellar space. No two such air masses are alike. Each has its own particular color and density, which change according to weather, time of day, and season of year, but whose general character derives from the climate and geology of the region. One of the most striking characteristics of a place or country is the color and quality of its enveloping air. Thus, for example, the summer sky low above the sea on the west coast of Morocco is usually a muddy purple, whereas on the coast of Maine on a bright summer day it is a bright blue green. And the milky sky of the Île-de-France can never be confused with the clear sky of Greece.

As an object recedes into the distance and sinks deeper into the mass of air, two changes take place in its appearance. Its local color becomes attenuated and loses its vivacity, while at the same time, its light-and-dark values are pulled together so that its modeling tends to flatten out. Each plane of distance in a landscape has its permissible range of color contrasts and value differences. And if an object in a picture is to appear to lie at a particular distance, both the lights and darks with which it is painted, and the color contrasts as well, must fit the range appropriate to this distance. Even the basic shape of objects changes according to distance. Objects like rocks or trees which are situated in a nearby plane appear distinct and sharply separated. In a more distant plane, where their apparent size is less and their value and color contrasts less, they cease to register as separate objects and reduce, in the middle distance, to details on a surface, and in the far distance, to a surface texture. There are many such details and textures to render when one is painting landscape, so that if a painter is to get everything at its right distance, and make his trees look like trees and his rocks like rocks whether near or far, he must deal with subtleties of tone and minutiae of detail quite outside the range of still life or figure painting, and must learn special techniques for doing it.

This is what I attempted in Chattanooga, and afterward in New Mexico and Vermont. New Mexico, with its vistas of plains and distant mountains, the rocks and earth in spectacular colors, and the air sparkling with a thin, dry dust, was different from anything I had ever seen, so different that I was sure it would prove quite easy. It did not. New Mexico is a mineral realm, a lunar landscape with the grandeur of great size but without a trace of human occupation to animate it and give it poetry and meaning, without trees or houses, never a man and seldom a horse, nothing to relate it to human size and give it scale except an occasional line of fence posts snaking up a mesa side. And the landscapes I did there, with bright colors and strange rock formations, came out more like scenic backdrops for an empty stage than like oil painting. Vermont was better. The Vermont countryside has everything to give it scale—houses, barns, cattle, pastures, and plowed fields. But the lush northern summer landscape seemed very foreign to me, too tidy and too green, brought up as I had been in the baked, untidy South. Eventually I got some pictures out of it, but always as a tourist. I was never able to take possession of the land and put my mark on it as I had learned to do in the South where I felt at home.

After this, I painted in north Florida, staying with friends who owned a plantation there. It was a country of pale, gnat-infested, sandy plains, the sparsely cultivated fields cut by pine flats and hammocks of live oaks, with scattered farmhouses of unpainted wood baked by the sun to the color of a worn and dirty silver dollar. Here the landscape problem was much simpler. There were no vistas, for the land traveled off flat into the distance, and the huge oaks and rickety houses were better suited to the portrait-cum-still-life approach to landscape which I was following than were the Western deserts or the damp New England meadows.

The light was usually veiled and somewhat sad. The earth was a creamy, almost white, sand color and the sky a washed-out blue. (Henry James somewhere describes Florida as having a weak charm.) The foliage of the live oaks was so dead a tone that it was scarcely green. The cataracts of dove-gray Spanish moss (a relative, I am told, of the pineapple) which dripped from their interpenetrating branches changed after a heavy rain to a muddy, Art Nouveau olive. The absence of bright color led me to simplify my palette. Everything here could be painted with only white, black, the earth colors, naples yellow, prussian blue along with a little cobalt for the skies—a Late Romantic palette for what was essentially a Romantic subject. I had given up my tempera underpainting; I had learned to block in a composition without it, certainly a safer procedure. The effect got by oppositions of warms and colds was particularly useful when it came to painting the complex pendants of moss, whose spidery interlacings I found could be brought into relief and moulded into vistas and recesses by ever so tiny a change from buff to slate. I worked hard at these particular effects, and I believe I achieved them, though they are scarcely visible in those pictures today. The differences of warm and cold which served to separate the planes of moss were too slight to survive the inevitable yellowing which affects oil paint as it grows older. If I were painting these pictures now, I would know from experience to make the differences of tone much sharper.

These oaks with their veils of moss were interesting enough to keep me at them for several years (Fig. 49). They were the last pictures I did by the system I had taken from Cézanne, of beginning at the edges of the forms and painting from the edges in. The drapings of moss and their sober colors must have made the pictures seem rather moody, for though my dealer liked them, few of them were sold. One of them—a large, complicated wood interior with tree stumps interwound with grapevines—I myself took an intense dislike to without knowing why. At the time I was at work on this particular picture, my farmer friends were doing a great deal of rabbit hunting and it usually fell to me to skin and dress the rabbits. Not until some years later did I discover that instead of the knotted roots and coils of vine, which I had intended to put down, I had in reality made an accurate depiction, even to the color, of the clammy entrails and naked haunches which I had found so repulsive to handle. And I was forced to admit that whatever may be the ostensible subject of a picture, its real subject is the life the painter is leading and how he feels about it. In a commissioned work like a portrait, this is not necessarily so. But in a landscape or a still life, which follow no directive except the painter's own needs and pleasure, the principle holds exactly. The choice of subject matter may be governed by all sorts of outside considerations. What the painter puts into it derives from his interior life. To look into this farther, let us see what sorts of landscape subjects the painter has chosen in the past.

Landscape as an independent branch of painting dates, in the West at any rate, from fairly recent times. There are many landscape motifs in Roman mosaics and Pompeian frescoes. But these houses and trees and riverbanks are not true landscapes. They appear either as decorative elements or as background for figures. In the Middle Ages, landscape found a similar use as a setting for Biblical stories or the doings of saints. Even in the Renaissance, landscape remained a sort

Fig. 49. MAURICE GROSSER, Florida Oak Trees, circa 1950. *Artist's Collection.*

of stage-set backdrop for portraits, battles, classical myths, and Christian legends. Often, however, the landscape background rather than the anecdote is pushed into importance, as in Magnasco, where a huge and detailed wilderness becomes the foil for one tiny saint (Fig. 50), or as in Brueghel, where vast stretches of sea and mountain leave only an inconspicuous corner for Icarus's fall. There are exceptions to this, of course. El Greco's *View of Toledo,* in the New York Metropolitan, comes at once to mind. But even as late as Claude Lorrain, landscape usually excused itself behind some literary or poetic pretext. It was not, really, until the middle of the seventeenth century and in Holland that landscape began to be a distinct species of painting sufficient in itself, when prosperous Dutch merchants leading sedentary lives found that one could use a picture of the out-of-doors, of boats and sea and fields, to act as a window to bring fresh air and light into a stuffy office. Later on, in the eighteenth century, another class of clients for landscape appeared which greatly increased the demand. These were the noble lords and young gentlemen doing the grand tour of Europe and putting the final international polish on their education. These rich and cultivated travelers required souvenir views of the places they had visited; some of them even brought their private watercolorists along with them in their suites. Photography had not yet been invented, but there were plenty of competent painters to do its work, and painters like Guardi and Canaletto and Bellotto furnished these new clients with views of the celebrated cities in picture-postcard quantities. The paintings they provided were frankly souvenirs, as were also the engravings of monuments by Piranesi, or on a cheaper scale, the *vues d'optique* which furnished less pretentious mementos of ruins and palaces. Thus, landscape as a separate kind of painting seems to begin here as souvenirs and documentation. At any rate, the earliest independent landscape studies I know of, the marvelous drawings made by Leonardo of air currents and cloud formations in the Arno Valley (Fig. 51), are factual documents.

Landscape very soon outgrew this subservient role. The Romantic poets discovered the emotional impact of the pathetic fallacy, which lends human emotions to inanimate things, so that in their writings, mountains can threaten, the sky frown, and the sea rise up in anger. Such personification furnished landscape painting with a new kind of subject which exhibited nature in her dramatic moods. Romantic painters like the English John Martin, in pictures like *The Destruction of Tyre* (Fig. 52) or *The Fall of Babylon* in which the sky rains fire and the waves smite, were able to paint the wilder aspects of nature and make very effective use of them. The Romantic poets with their love of the

Fig. 50. MAGNASCO, Monks in Landscape. *Collection Mr. and Mrs. John Koch.*

189

Fig. 51. LEONARDO DA VINCI, A Cloudburst.
Reproduced by Gracious Permission of Her Majesty Queen Elizabeth II.

190

Fig. 52. JOHN MARTIN, The Destruction of Tyre. *The Toledo Museum of Art, Toledo, Ohio. Gift of Edward Drummond Libbey, 1952.*

exotic also inspired painters to travel. And there arose a class of painter-travelers like Turner and Edward Lear whose subject matter was the distant, the foreign, the picturesque, done indeed as souvenir views, but at the same time with the Romantic coloration of a visionary world glimpsed by the poet in his solitude.

For us today, this is all a little too literary. The Romantic soul has long gone out of fashion. More to our taste is the French good sense of Corot which would have nothing to do with it. Even the groves with their nymphs which Corot did in his late years defer more to Poussin than to Romantic imagery. His early Roman pictures are so little Romantic that they might be taken as souvenir views made for a discriminating eighteenth-century market. And the French landscapes that compose the major part of his work are not Romantic either. They are a straightforward rendering of the pleasant views a painter would come upon in a pretty and not particularly distinguished countryside. The distinction they exhibit does not derive from any unusual or striking subject matter, but only from the skill and delicacy of the hand that made them.

Even the Impressionists kept to the same sort of subject. Despite their elaborate technique designed on the latest theories of color and vision to show what the world really looked like, the world their pictures described was still the world of Corot, the comfortable, unremarkable middle-class world of France before the wars. And no matter how much the painters of the time were influenced by Japanese prints and Japanese methods of composition, none of them thought to go to Japan and paint there. Of all the well-known ones, only Gauguin, a desperate man, went far afield to take exotic subjects. The exotic and the picturesque were too closely connected with an outmoded Romanticism to be possible. The subject of these pre–World War painters, from Boudin and Chase down to young Derain and Glackens, reduces to the quite ordinary views a painter would have encountered walking in his native city or in the pleasant and not very picturesque places where he would have gone to pass the summer.

After the 1914–1918 war, all this was changed. The quiet middle-class domesticity which Impressionism had illustrated became an unacceptable subject for landscape or for anything else. Landscape became urban and replete with social consciousness. Georgia O'Keeffe and John Marin took on the New York skyline; Hopper painted the suburbs. Painters turned to abnormal psychology to produce the dislocated villages of Soutine and the dream perspectives of Dali, and Eugène Berman began to devote himself to the decay of cities. With the depression, abnormality, poverty, and decay became so highly regarded that Man Ray could think it proper to boast, quite mistakenly I believe, that all good

American art is done on lousy subject matter. A few painters like Léonid kept on with the normal subject matter of Corot and Boudin but removed the undesirable middle-class associations from the pictures by making them of distant and unfrequented places inhabited by the nonunionized poor, such as shepherds and fishermen.

Today, with the social violence of the world around us no longer hidden, social consciousness has become as unacceptable a subject as middle-class comfort was in the 'twenties and 'thirties, whereas the quiet life of the years before the wars has taken on the romantic and wistful charm of something pleasant which has disappeared. Painters like Fairfield Porter or Picasso, living quietly in the country, can again busy themselves depicting the background of their domestic life. Along with this, urbanism has become so unpleasant and even so shocking a subject that it is either passed over in silence or exhibited in noisy glee. No landscape painter is willing to touch it. Georgia O'Keeffe today would not think of painting a skyscraper, or Hopper, if he were alive, a modern supermarket. Now that countryside is turning rapidly into suburb, what is above all inacceptable and shocking in a pictured landscape is any hint of modern architecture or of suburban living, of poured concrete or moulded plastic or any of the nationally advertised products associated with them. On the other hand, the shock value of this urban and suburban material is one of the chief reasons for Pop Art's great success, at least its great success with the museums. Shock value and news value are most important for commending a contemporary work to museum purchase. And Pop Art, with its systematic use of such forbidden subject matter, certainly today possesses both.

The taboo on suburban material, however, is probably as transitory as any other stricture and is perhaps only a question of a particular age group. The vulgarities we lived with as a child we find homely and touching. Only the vulgarities which we encounter later on seem ugly and depressing. The Pop Art painters are of a generation for which advertising slogans have probably the same tender childhood associations that Cecil Beaton, for example, finds in the Edwardian fashions of his youth. Certainly the singing commercials of the 'thirties, "Pepsi Cola hits the spot," and so on, have already taken on a nostalgic poetry, even for "squares." Quite independent of whether one approves of it or not, Pop Art can be defined as a school of painting, even of landscape painting, which takes suburbia as its subject. Just as Diaz took for his subject the oak trees around the village where he spent his summers, and Monet, the water lilies of the pond across the railroad tracks from his garden, so also the Pop Artist paints the super-market interiors and oversized billboards which form the familiar landscape background of his daily living.

As one can see from this hasty summary, the painter of landscape has taken at one time or another almost every possible aspect of nature as his subject. But whether his intention was to open a window, to provide a souvenir view, or to present a storm at sea, to record a nightmare vision, or to describe the quiet background of a Sunday walk, the real and basic subject is a poetic image—something he has seen or imagined and which he can remember with pleasure or tenderness or dread. This image must be quite clear in the painter's mind before he begins to paint, and it will be evident and complete in even the roughest kind of preliminary sketch, where one is always surprised to find that the most incomprehensible scribble will turn out, in the light of the finished work, to have had a precise, if shorthand, meaning. In fact, the clear perception of this image is what first impelled him to undertake the picture. And the clearer the image is to him, the easier the picture will be to paint. The lasting value of the work, the length of time it can continue to hold our interest, depends on the skill and knowledge with which the work is painted. But whatever carrying power the work possesses, whatever ability to attract the eye and remain fixed in the memory, comes from the vitality and clarity of the poetic image and from nothing else.

The source of this image is an intimacy the painter has established with the place he is painting, a condensation of his feelings and perceptions about it, the same sort of intimacy he would establish with a portrait sitter. In this, landscape painting is very like portrait painting, with the difference that in landscape painting, the *genius loci* himself is on the model stand. To get his likeness, the painter needs a special insight, derived perhaps from some knowledge of the place's history, or from a feeling for its inhabitants acquired in living with them or sleeping with them or playing other games. And, just as a portrait painter tries to keep away from outright caricature, the landscape painter must firmly avoid the picturesque. He is not a tourist for whose camera the picturesque is the best of subject matters. On the contrary, the painter can deal with the picturesque only when he has learned to disregard its strangeness and join it onto the things he already knows, until it has become an indistinguishable part of his own internal landscape, a landscape which, no matter how commonplace the painter himself may find it, is to everybody else the most picturesque thing there is.

As one can see, painting a landscape has a great deal more to it than simply rendering a view. And even if it were only this, the painter would still be better at it than the camera. Because our criterion for reality is what we ourselves see. And what we see and what the camera sees are not at all the same. When we see, our eyes take in the outside world as a series of tiny, fragmentary images seen in rapid succession, which our memory and our binocular vision then take and weld into a unified whole. So that the view the painter looks at as he paints has already been organized by his mind to fit into a four-dimensional continuum—up-and-down, right-and-left, near-and-far, and motion. The camera, on the other hand, sees the whole view at a glance, instantly, without extension in time, and from a single point of view. The world it presents is a world of two dimensions, an instantaneous cross-section, without depth or movement. The two ways of seeing have very little in common, and it would be very illogical to confuse them. Besides this, the camera has great faults when it comes to seeing color. No color film can properly record color when there are great differences of luminosity such as, say, between a white wall in sunlight and a blue dress in shadow, color and value differences which the eye does see and which the painter can record, if he must, by using rather simple tricks. More serious than this, the colors which one gets when a color film is processed are quite unpredictable. They are the result of immensely complicated factors—the kind of film, the conditions under which it was stored, the length of the exposure, and the color of the light the picture was taken by, as well as the inevitable small variations in the time of development and the freshness and temperature of the developing baths—circumstances too numerous and too fortuitous to control.

To say that the color of a photograph is accidental, however, does not condemn it as a photograph. All photographs are the result of accident. A good photographer is one who knows how to take advantage of the accidents and has the eye and taste to discard all photographs save those which, by happy accident, present a striking image. These images are often very startling indeed, because the photograph, being a cross section of time, can catch and arrest the movement of crowds, of bodies, of faces, the way no painter can. Just the same, no matter how vivid the photographic image may be, it cannot hold the eyes as a painting can. Even the beautiful landscape photographs of such a skilled technician as Ansel Adams, if hung on a wall and kept there, will in no time at all grow tiresome to look at and then invisible. The details of the image are made up of small particles lined up on a thin film by chemical means. A surface such as this cannot have the depth and variety and purposeful complexity of a hand-painted surface, and it cannot continue long to hold the spectator's interest. But an even graver fault is that the photographic image has no inherent scale such as a painting always has.

A photograph is made by the projection of a bundle of light rays through a lens. Its details have been put in their places without the use of muscular tensions, without any stress on hand or arm, and there is no reason except convenience why it should have any particular size. But with a painting, its size bears a necessary relation to the use to which it is to be put and to the amount of effort and detailed work that went into making it. This relation of the size of the picture to the size of the subject it represents is what is known as the picture's scale, a relation which, as I shall explain in Chapter 12, cannot be changed without changing the picture's character, and has a great deal to do in determining the value and beauty of the work as well as the particular effect it has on us.

But the most serious of all its faults is that the camera cannot exercise a choice. All details that fall within its range of vision are put down exactly as they are seen. The camera cannot select among them, or rearrange them for balance and emphasis as a painter does. The camera examines nature through a stationary peephole and for a single instant of time. Its gets lost in the details of the subject and cannot disentangle the structure and patterns of space and shapes which the painter sees in it. When I first acquired a Leica, I used to take photographs of all the landscape subjects I was working on, thinking that they would come in handy later if there were any retouching to be done. But the photographs always turned out so little like the scene which I remembered painting that I was never able to use any of them. And no matter how well the painting itself came out, the photograph itself was never very interesting. Indeed, it was often difficult to conceive from looking at it how any painting would have been engendered by so tedious a subject. The fact is that the painter, with his binocular vision and sense of space and depth, has started off from quite a different image. And he is able to add and subtract details, change accents, shift lines, values, colors, and everything else till the image comes out clear.

I recently came upon a handsome book on the French ballet* in which a large section is devoted to Picasso's work with Diaghilev in Italy in the early 'twenties. Included among the illustrations and placed on facing pages are a drawing and a photograph. The drawing is one of Picasso's most famous ones, of Diaghilev together with his manager Salisburg, two plump, well-shaved men in top hats and evening dress, one sitting in a chair, the other standing. It is done in the celebrated wire-hard, continuous, unaccented line one finds in other Picasso drawings of the period, such as the well-known portrait drawings of

* *Le Ballet en France.* Boris Kochno. Paris: Hachette, 1954.

Satie and Stravinsky. On the facing page is the photograph from which the drawing was derived. It would appear, from the identity of every contour in the two illustrations, that the drawing is nothing but a tracing from the photograph. However reprehensible it might be thought to pass off such an easy trick as a skilled exercise in freehand drawing, it still remains that the drawing, even if it is derivative, has a carrying power and a clarity of intention which the photograph with all its pretention to realism does not possess. The drawing, tracing though it may be, was made by hand.

· 12 ·

THE PALETTE KNIFE
SCALE · CANVAS
VARNISH · TURPENTINE
FRAMES

LÉONID, WHO ALWAYS seemed to me willfully ignorant about any but the most standard techniques of painting, had very definite ideas how painting should be done and never approved of the way I went about it. He scolded me, insisting, and he was right, that painting is not drawing (Cézanne had insisted that it was not sculpture either), that color is more important than either line or shading, and that proper color cannot be got by indiscriminately rubbing paint on the canvas like smudges of charcoal, as he accused me of doing. Each tone in a picture, he said, must be a distinct and definite thing, a precise shade of paint with identity and weight. Even an unimportant transition tone for shadows must have more character than only that of being right in value and not too far off in hue. It must be a real color which could be mixed up again to match if it is needed. He maintained, in sum, that every tone used in a picture must be a recognizable color, not an indefinite effect got by rubbing one thing over another

---

or by smearing things together. All this sounded very reasonable to me. But I had got into the habit of mixing each brushload of color separately as I came to need it out of whatever I found lying on the palette, and Léonid's ideas would not fit into my rather slipshod working methods.

One fall in New York just after the war, I decided that I needed some practice in figure drawing and enrolled at the Art Students League in an afternoon course in figure drawing conducted by the painter Edwin Dickinson. Most of the students were recently demobilized GI's, new to art school. I suspect they were attracted more by the presence of nude models than by any real desire to learn to paint, because whenever the model, who was changed every week, was fat or male, I had the class all to myself. But Dickinson was very gentle with us all and very courteous. Only once did I see him lose his patience and this with a student who was beginning a four-foot canvas by drawing in the model's eyelashes with a tiny sable brush. Dickinson snatched the boy's brush from him and handed him a sliver of broken shingle instead. "She doesn't need eyelashes," he said, "She needs color. Mix the color with this stick. Hold it up to the model to see if you have got it right. Then use the stick to put it on the canvas where it belongs. It doesn't matter how much it slops over the edge as long as it is the right value and the right color."

This was exactly what Léonid had been telling me all along. Hearing it expressed again, and this time so forcibly, impressed me with its very good sense, all except the part about the piece of shingle. If one used a palette knife instead, one would have a quite practical way of painting. I tried it and found that I was in possession of the best and easiest way I had ever encountered for getting good, clear color. This is how one goes about it.

Suppose one wishes to mix the colors for painting a piece of drapery or for the gradations of a sky. For each separate tone in the subject—for that part of the drapery which faces the light, say, or for the section of sky above a particular group of trees—one takes the knife and mixes a tone of paint to match, holds up the knife so that the paint on the blade can be compared directly with the color in nature one is attempting to match, and adjusts the paint mixture until the two colors are indistinguishable one from the other. When preparing tones of color in this way, one must be careful always to hold the blade at the same angle and in the same light; otherwise nothing will come out right. The principal colors for the picture should all be made up before one starts to paint and should be aligned on the palette in some sort of order. This is very important, for when the tones of paint are laid on the palette, they look very little like the colors one remembers having set out to match. Besides this, the various tones for painting a particular passage—of drapery, say, or sky—once on the palette all look so much alike that unless they are kept in order, one can never remember which is which. When the tones have been made up, they can be put on with a brush, or applied directly to canvas with the knife itself, a very useful tool indeed for covering large surfaces rapidly.

All this must be kept very flexible. Above all, one should never let the palette become unmanageably crowded. A new tone can be prepared very quickly when one comes to need it, and any tone which gets used up can always be mixed again. Just the same, the principal colors which will be used throughout the painting should be prepared in large enough quantities to last. They can be kept fresh indefinitely if one protects them from the air by putting them under water between painting sessions, or simply by covering them with pieces of aluminum foil. Mixing up enough color is particularly desirable when one is painting things, like clouds or sea or sky, which change from day to day. A sky, for that matter, changes color from minute to minute; a tone which matched at ten o'clock will no longer match at ten thirty. And a tone of paint one prepares on a subsequent day to mend a flaw in a previously painted sky, even though the color may seem to blend perfectly when wet, will always dry to stand out as a distressingly visible blemish.

This way of mixing tones of paint and comparing them with the corresponding tones in nature removes any vagueness one might have in distinguishing warms from colds. In fact, it turns the warm-and-cold relation into a so definite and measureable thing that one no longer needs the artificial aid of verbal tags to make one see it. One also discovers in matching colors with the knife that our instinctive sense of color recognition and color naming is quite unreliable, for the tones of paint one gets in this way are usually quite unlike what one had imagined in advance. The blue of the sky invariably turns out to be less blue than one had thought, and white walls are never white but assume the most unexpected and illogical shadings of green and orange and violet.

The method has one tiny disadvantage; it wastes a great deal of paint. When a tone goes wrong in mixing, as it so frequently does, comes out too dark, or too dull, or too tan, it can always be saved by the addition of more paint. But by the time it has been made right, it will usually have built up into much more of this particular color than one could possibly use. Also, if one employs the knife for painting as well as for mixing colors, the paint goes on much thicker than with a brush and gets used up much faster. The method is also extravagant in palette knives. The best knives are Italian imports, handmade and no two alike. Besides, they change a great deal with use, becoming much more supple, and it is impossible to tell by handling them in the shop which ones are any good. So one is forced to buy a great many to find a knife one likes. The better the knife, the more brittle it seems to be. Invariably at the most critical point of a painting, the favorite instrument will snap in two and one is forced to bring out a new, stiff, unfamiliar one and break it in. But it is all well worth the trouble. A good knife can be made to do almost anything, from putting down a tiny fleck of color to filling a large area. It can paint a sharp edge and even draw a reasonably thin line, though line and modeling and fine detail are, naturally enough, easier with a brush. The brush, on the other hand, does not keep the colors nearly so clean. The bristles always retain some traces of a preceding color, which inescapably soils the color one is now using. Whereas the blade of a knife can be wiped instantly clean. The knife can also be made to give extraordinarily rich textures. The rocks and foliage of Courbet's woodland pictures could not have been done without it. Yet the obvious palette-knife effects, such as parallel veinings of unmixed colors, and smooth patches of paint with heavy upturned edges like trowel marks, always appear slovenly and are best avoided. In fact, the knife is acceptable as an instrument for painting only when its use cannot be detected.

The first time I was able to put all this to serious use was on a trip to Greece. My dealer, Alexander Iolas, who had shown my Florida tree pictures in his New York gallery, was a Greek, and his enthusiasm for his native land, along with my own memories of the Greek and Latin classics of my school days, persuaded me to go and try to paint there (Fig. 53). And in Greece I found the knife indispensable. Holding up a tone of paint before the eye and comparing it with the colors of the land turned out to be a much more serviceable way of recording the effects of air and distance, of sunlight and shadow, than the linear approach to painting I had inherited from Cézanne, and perfect for transcribing the clear Hellenic light.

One of the greatest charms of landscape painting lies in the unmistakable way it can describe the character of a country. In such evocation, actual details of topography play very little part. The real and effectual elements are the peculiar and characteristic colors of the country's rocks and soil and foliage, and the way these colors are changed and harmonized by the quality of sunlight that falls on them, and by the color of the air which bathes them. And the only practical way I know for exploring such subtleties is to compare each tone of paint with the colors in the subject. For me, this means doing it on the spot. My memory

Fig. 53. MAURICE GROSSER, House in Hydra, 1954. *Robert Hull Fleming Museum, Burlington, Vermont.*

of the colors in a landscape is never clear enough to enable me to bring them back to the studio unchanged. And there is no color notation which can record a precise tone of color in any terms except as an imprecise and verbalized average. Consequently, I am compelled to set my easel up in front of the motif and work from nature.

I am aware that I speaking here of something that has now gone out of fashion. Professional painters no longer paint out-of-doors. The watercolorist you see seated in a field—and so rarely now—will certainly be an amateur. Landscapes, almost without exception, are made up in the studio. Léonid composes at home, depending less on drawings or sketches than on his extraordinary visual memory. And a controversy in the papers a few years back, on the origin of a figure in one of Walter Stuempfig's beach scenes, showed that even Stuempfig painted from photographs, as indeed did Degas. In fact, so little painting is done out-of-doors today that it has become impossible to buy a practical landscape easel. There are plenty of light, ingenious contraptions to be had for sketching while seated, but nothing can be found which is either strong enough or tall enough for serious work. The sturdy *chevalet belge,* once standard equipment for all landscape painters, is no longer manufactured, and nothing can be had which will take its place. It was a very simple machine—seven pieces of strong hardwood, two metal clamps to hold the bottom of the canvas, and a three foot metal bar to clamp and hold the top of it. It was tall enough to paint at standing up, would take anything from a tiny panel to a canvas one four feet tall, and lift the bottom of the canvas up to where it could be worked on at eye level. I had the great luck to have a *chevalet belge* left over from Paris days. I had made a triangle of plywood which fitted between the legs and served as painting table, so that I did not have to hold a palette and had both hands free for working. I had also a three-armed brace which screwed to the legs and held the whole thing firm. And by using a rock to act as ballast, I could keep a canvas steady enough to paint even in quite windy weather.

Indeed, weather is one of the landscape painter's most stubborn problems. He must cope with wind which shakes his canvas and with rain which melts its priming, with seasons that change and with weeks of storms that come on just as he is on the point of finishing an important picture. Even cloudy days are troublesome. A cloudy day is often more beautiful than a sunny one. The light is softer and more varied, and the shifting clouds give depth and drama to the sky, and their shadows on fields and mountains point up and underline the different planes of distance. But no two cloudy days are alike. All sunny days are more or less the same, and much more suitable for pictures which will take more than one sitting to complete. Now that I was becoming a confirmed landscape painter, it seemed simpler to keep away from the northern countries with their irregular weather patterns, and confine myself to the Mediterranean basin where sunny weather lasts all summer, and where tan, not green, is the dominating color of the land—southern Spain, North Africa, Sicily, Greece, in short the outposts of the Roman Empire, which my Classical education had particularly fitted me to understand. I was afraid that the bright Mediterranean light might be hard on the eyes, and I bought some dark-gray sunglasses to use while painting, thinking that the gray would deform all the colors equally, and that the tones I had matched while wearing glasses would continue to match when I took the glasses off. For a while this seemed to work, though the blue of my skies tended to turn a little heavy. Then the glasses got stolen. I replaced them by others as near like them as I could find. But they were not the same, for the pictures painted with the new glasses on always seemed muddy and dead when I got them home. Disquieted by this, I took one of the pictures back to where I had painted it and compared it to the subject itself. As long as I had glasses on, the picture looked right and luminous and the colors true. Seen without the glasses, most of the values turned out to be false and all the colors dirty. To save the picture, I was obliged to repaint it tone by tone. After this, I reserved dark glasses for driving and got a big straw hat, which protected my eyes even better from the sun and did not deform the colors.

Here in the Mediterranean basin I came on a device which I was to use and profit by for many years—reducing the scale of a large landscape subject to make it fit a tiny canvas. I already knew about enlarging the scale of things; I had practiced it on the fruit in still lifes. But I had not before tried making the scale smaller.

Scale, which I have already mentioned in connection with photography, is a major factor in determining the character of a work of art. Scale has to do with the actual sizes involved in making the work and how they compare with the size of a human being. To put it more precisely, scale is a set of arithmetical proportions in three terms. The first term is the size of the picture itself; the second is the size of the details and objects which compose the picture; the third term, which is the basic one, is the size of our own body. This unit of five feet four to six feet two is the unit we are forced to use for measuring anything that affects our motor senses or excites our emotions, and is the fundamental element in any artistic judgment. It explains, for example, why a picture in a private house always seems grander than if we had come upon it in a museum. In a museum, the large, impersonal emptiness of the hall where it is hung takes away the work's real size to make it look small and somewhat unimportant. Whereas in the more intimate interior of a private house, the domestic proportions of the rooms, and the familiar sizes of the furniture in them, make us immediately aware how big the picture actually is compared to our own body. And if the picture is a big and handsome one, it becomes extremely impressive. This also is why one can never get a just idea of the character of a work of art from a color slide or photograph of it: because the photograph, having no built-in scale, can tell us nothing of the work's real size.

If the actual size of a picture is an important element in the impression it makes on us, the size of the objects in it and the sizes of the details and brushwork used in painting these objects are important elements as well. Let us take up first the size of detail and brushwork.

Suppose we are standing in front of the picture in question and so can comprehend its actual size by measuring it against our own. Then the size of its details and brushwork take on for us a real and effective emotional connotation. For, though we are probably not consciously aware of it, we cannot help but feel our own body pull in sympathy with the body movements the painter used, and the muscular tensions he felt, when working to make brushstrokes and details of that particular size. The effect on us, the spectators, may be subliminal, but it is very real. The New York Abstract Expressionist painters for example, like Kline or de Kooning, depend for a good deal of their effect on the sympathetic muscular tensions they hope to arouse by their brushstrokes, so obviously produced by large, free movements of the painter's wrist and shoulder. The showy Action Painter Mathieu, in fact, called particular attention to this by giving press conferences where he would be photographed as he stabbed and parried and lunged at his canvas, dressed in the costume of a Japanese swordsman. Such effects are more familiar to us, and perhaps more legitimately exploited, in Chinese art calligraphy and in the Chinese and Japanese painting styles allied to it.

The size at which objects are shown in a picture is perhaps even more important than the size of detail or brushstroke. A painter at work usually stands within arm's length—a little nearer than this, say eighteen to twenty inches if the work is highly detailed, and at three or four feet if he is painting broadly. This painter-to-canvas distance normally determines the size which things are drawn; it is easiest to give an object the size that it would assume on the canvas if the canvas itself were transparent, like a primitive form of *camera obscura,* and the painter were seeing the object through it. The normal and expected size of a portrait head, for example, is three-quarters life-size. If the head is drawn either noticeably larger or smaller than this norm, the spectator is aware of an added tension, which indeed the painter himself felt when working in this un-accustomed scale, a tension which changes the expressive character of the work to make it much more striking. A new scale can be very useful for imposing a new and unexpected interpretation on a familiar subject. Just as an out-moded style of decoration can be dramatized and made visible again by an unexpected change of color—like covering brown Victorian woodwork with white paint or bleaching Spanish Mission fumed oak to blond. In the same way, a too familiar painting subject can be given a new stylishness and interest by presenting it in an un-familiar size.

Such change of scale for purely expressive reasons is fairly common. It was used by Georgia O'Keeffe for painting oversized flowers, and by Bérard and Tchelitchew for their oversized portrait heads. I myself had made use of it to render vegetables monumental. But I had not yet tried it out in a landscape. Painters, however have always done so, and I was aware how effective a small scale could be from Léonid's small seascapes and from the tiny Moroccan gouaches of Brion Gysin which condense into their minute compass all the details of nomad life, from sandstorms to bicycles (Fig. 54). I myself came onto it through the small preliminary sketches I was accustomed to make in planning a summer's work. Too many good subjects always turned up, and there was never time to make carefully worked-out paintings of them all. But one could always find time for a small canvas. The rapidity with which a small canvas could be painted—seldom requiring more than two or three sessions—helped give a fine unity of air and color, a unity much more difficult to sustain in a large work requiring a fortnight to complete. Beside this, I found it intensely interesting to see the amount of depth and distance which could be got into so small an area, and the amount of detail that could be implied without actually putting any of it down.

American stretchers, which do not come with sizes smaller than eight inches, were too big for such small paintings. I had to go into French sizes, called *numeros,* and I found these standardized shapes so pleasant to work with that I have used them consistently since.

No one knows when the French system was invented; certainly before the adoption of the centimeter in which its dimensions are now given, for in the

Fig. 54. BRION GYSIN, Arabs on the Place at Marrakesh. Wash drawing. *Collection of the Author.*

Mesures régulières des Toiles et Cadres

N°s	FIGURE	PAYSAGE	MARINE
00	16×12		
0	18×14	18×12	
1	22×16	22×14	22×12
2	24×19	24×16	24×14
3	27×22	27×19	27×16
4	33×24	33×22	33×19
5	35×27	35×24	35×22
6	41×33	41×27	41×24
8	46×38	46×33	46×27
10	55×46	55×38	55×33
12	61×50	61×46	61×38
15	65×54	65×50	65×46
20	73×60	73×54	73×50
25	81×65	81×60	81×54
30	92×73	92×65	92×60
40	100×81	100×73	100×65
50	116×89	116×81	116×73
60	130×97	130×89	130×81
80	146×114	146×97	146×89
100	162×130	162×114	162×97
120	195×130	195×114	195×97

(vertical margin text repeated between columns: THE PARIS AMERICAN ART C°)

CADRES EN BOIS SCULPTÉ
de toutes dimensions
toujours en magasin (excepté Marine)

Fig. 55. French numéro table.

seventeenth and eighteenth centuries, picture frames were already being made in standard *numero* sizes. Today there are some twenty *numeros* in common use, each size named after a number (Fig. 55). The numbers go consecutively from 0 to 6, and after that with skips—8, 10, 12, 15, and so on—to 120. The numbers, I am told, correspond to the prices a color merchant would charge for canvases— a No. 1 canvas would cost one *solde,* and so on. If this is true, the system is very old indeed. Each number comes in three different shapes, called *figure, paysage,* and *marine,* all having the same length but each of a different width. *Marine* is the narrowest, *paysage* is broader, and *figure* the broadest. All the dimensions seem quite arbitrary, but there is nevertheless this pattern: the *figure* shape of any size has the same width as the *paysage* of the next size up, and also of the *marine* of the next size above that, so that a No. 8 *figure*, a No. 10 *paysage,* and a No. 12 *marine,* though of different lengths, have all the same width. Apart from this small regularity, the changes from one size to another are so erratic, and the shapes themselves are so satisfactory to work with, that one cannot help thinking that they must be based on some forgotten mathematico-aesthetic rule of thumb for getting good proportions, perhaps even the famous Golden Section of antiquity. In Europe, where the system is current and both canvases and frames conform to it, framing pictures becomes somewhat easier than here because frames can generally be found already made up in all the common *numero* shapes and sizes.

Out of all this has grown a routine of painting which I have followed now for a number of years without any disagreeable consequences, and the pictures I have painted by it do not seem to crack or grow unduly dark or yellow. There are many other ways of painting which I am sure are equally safe. Edward Melcarth is quite satisfied with his way of working on a canvas prepared with gesso, using casein white, or a mixture of casein white and titanium in oil, for his underpainting, and overpainting and glazing with oil paint mixed with dammar varnish (Fig. 56). Such unalike painters as John Koch (See Fig. 37) and Fairfield Porter are quite happy with the Marogier medium. And Pietro Annigoni, portrait painter to the Queen of England, has a most beautiful, and I believe secret, method of working with tempera and glazes on rag paper glued to canvas. But here I intend to speak only of things I have used myself for many years and which I know from my own experience will work. The four or five pages which follow are all about working methods and recipes, things not particularly useful to the general reader but which may possibly interest him.

First, the canvas. One of the commonest mistakes of an inexperienced painter is to work on a canvas which has not been sufficiently primed. Prepared canvas, even from a good manufacturer, is seldom well enough primed to be able to take a clean brushstroke. And the painter who uses commercially prepared canvas usually finds that he must spend most of his first session in the purely mechanical labor of filling up the grain of the canvas so that it will take the paint. Almost any commercial canvas will be easier to paint on if it is first given a coat of gray or beige oil paint and left a few days to dry. This coat should be thinned, if necessary, with turpentine, not with oil. An excess of oil will give a slick surface on which the subsequent paint takes badly. The tone of the priming coat should be light. A dark priming is difficult to cover and to hide, and, besides, impels

Fig. 56. EDWARD MELCARTH, Manhole, 1959. *Collection Forbes.*

the painter to paint a dark picture. Oil paint always grows darker with time, and it is best to keep a picture light and clear from the beginning if one wishes to protect it from a heavy and impenetrable old age.

I myself no longer use commercial canvas. I have been in the habit for many years of preparing my own canvases and find them a great deal more satisfactory than any I can buy. One gets good unbleached linen, which one cuts to shape and tacks on stretchers, pulling it as even and as taut as possible. Then, it is wet with water, allowed to dry, and restretched. A glue size is made up—about two ounces of sheet glue, or rabbit-skin glue, is put to soak in a quart of water and left till it swells up and becomes soft. The water is gently heated without letting it come to a boil, and stirred till the glue has dissolved. The stretched canvas is then given two coats of this; the second should not be applied until the first has dried. Between the coats the canvas is lightly sandpapered to remove any project-ing knots or threads. Then one takes white-lead paint, either artists' color straight from the tube or a good commercial white-lead paste, and smears it over the sur-face of the canvas with a palette knife, getting the paint well into the grain, and scraping off all the excess so that the canvas weave is everywhere visible. This is allowed to dry for a day or two, and on top of it another similar coat is given, and then perhaps a third, depending on how smooth a surface one desires. The final coat is made with paint toned to a silvery gray with black and yellow ocher. All this I generally plan on doing in the early spring, preparing a series of canvases in useful sizes which I try to keep from using till the fall, by which time they will probably be quite dry enough to work on. If they are left to season till the follow-ing spring, there will be even less danger of their cracking.

Canvases prepared in this way with only white-lead and glue are remark-ably tough and flexible. Pictures painted on them can be taken off their stretchers at the end of summer, rolled around a cardboard tube to make a package which will fit under the arm—this is perfectly safe as long as the canvas is rolled with the picture side out—and can be taken home as hand luggage, even in a plane. Once home, the pictures can be unrolled and tacked on other stretchers, and all without the bother and expense of packing and without the delay and dangers of shipping.

I usually begin a picture by sketching on the canvas with a brush dipped in paint thinned with turpentine, which one can easily erase and change with a rag or brush dipped in more turpentine. Recently I have got in the habit of beginning with a drawing in charcoal, which I then fix by tracing over the lines with a brush and thin paint. One must be careful to brush away all the remaining charcoal dust, which would dirty the subsequent paint and render the edges of the forms grimy and difficult to manipulate.

The principal tones in a picture, for sky, sea, earth, and so on, I try to have already prepared before beginning to paint. The large, even areas of the canvas I generally put on with a knife or with a broad, square sable brush. For the rest of the work I use sometimes bristle brushes, sometimes the knife, and, for fine details and textures "miniature" brushes, which are short, conical, sable brushes made for painting miniatures on ivory and sold, as far as I know, only by Winsor & Newton. In all this, I try to use as little painting medium as possible, usually only turpentine, but if the paint needs to be rendered more flexible for small details, turpentine mixed with linseed oil. But for the most part, I work only with turpentine, mixing very little of it with the colors and using it principally to keep the brushes clean. The turpentine should be the best—clear, white, and fragrant, and should not dry sticky when tried between thumb and forefinger. Formerly, double-distilled turpentine was available, but I have not seen it for some years, and the turpentine sold in small bottles at artists'-supply shops is generally not much better than commercial gum turpentine. This, when fresh, is usually quite acceptable. But it should be "gum" turpentine, not "steam distilled." This last is made by high-pressure distillation of old pine stumps and contains all sorts of gums and fractions. In Nigeria, where I painted winter before last, turpentine was not available, and I had to use what is called mineral spirits. It was not as fragrant as turpentine, but it worked well and dried without leaving a residue, which even the best turpentine seldom does.

I never use driers. The white lead which I use for white is itself a drier and causes everything to dry quite fast enough, so that a picture is generally dry enough the next day to be taken up again. This for me is important, because I like to keep on with the same picture day after day until it is done, and try to finish everything on the spot. Whatever final retouching there is to do, I do later at home, when the season's work is done and the pictures are all together. Before retouching a work, it is best to wipe it clean with a soft, clean, moist rag. This takes off the summer's accumulation of dust and helps remove the chalky spots which some of the tones, particularly the blues, exhibit in drying. These will all normally disappear when the picture is varnished, and one should never try to remove them by rubbing them with linseed oil. A film of linseed oil put on transparently darkens and yellows a great deal more than the same oil would do when mixed in with the paint. And oil rubbed on a painting to freshen it up will invariably turn in aging to a dirty brown. Retouching varnishes I distrust and have never used. They are necessary only when one paints consistently in very dark tones, which I seldom do. As for the final varnishing, it should be put off as long as possible. Formerly, painters would wait till the very day the pictures were put up on exhibit, hence the word *vernissage* or "varnishing day."

The safest final varnish is probably gum dammar dissolved in spirits of turpentine; at any rate it is the one most painters in this country use. There are various plastic resins available which can be dissolved to make picture varnishes which are water-clear. One in particular, N-butyl methacrylate polymer, is soluble in turpentine. This I suspect is the only one of them we dare use. The solvents needed to dissolve the others are dangerously strong, strong enough to soften and dissolve even a well-dried picture surface. N-butyl methacrylate has apparently all the good qualities of dammar without having dammar's straw-colored tone. But it is difficult to find; few color merchants have it in stock. And it has the disadvantage of giving a very glassy surface.

All varnishes, however, are more or less glassy, particularly on a dark picture. A varnish put on thinly enough not to shine, will not be thick enough to render the surface of the picture uniform or strong enough to protect it. A coat of varnish must be heavy enough to shield the picture from dirt. What a picture restorer does when he cleans a picture is to remove the old varnish with its imbedded dirt and replace it with a new one. For this reason one should varnish only with what is called a spirit varnish, a light resin dissolved in turpentine, which a restorer can remove easily without disturbing the paint underneath. Tough oil-based varnishes like copal, which dry by the oxidation of an oil and not by the evaporation of a solvent, should be avoided. They go bad just as quickly as the spirit varnishes and can be removed only by very strong solvents which may also dissolve the picture.

Most of the dirt that accumulates on a picture is a residue from smoke, partly city and partly cigarette, and is fairly easy to get off without a drastic cleaning. A few tablespoons of vinegar, or a drop of a liquid household detergent, in a glass of water, a clean rag moistened with this, wrung dry, and then wiped over the picture with even strokes, then the same thing done over again, this time with clear water, will usually remove a smoke film and make the picture look a great deal brighter. Soap and water, or a very wet rag, should not be used. A serious cleaning or repair job on a valuable picture should be entrusted only to a professional restorer.

A dent caused by something hitting the canvas can be flattened out by moistening the back of the canvas at that spot and tightening the canvas by driving in the stretcher keys. A more serious dent or crease can be removed by taking the canvas off its stretcher, laying it on its face on a smooth surface, and moistening and ironing out the dent. One must take care that the iron is not hot enough to scorch the paint. A small tear in a picture is not difficult to mend, as long as the tear is not too big and the canvas backing is otherwise sound. The picture is laid on its face on a piece of clean paper and the edges of the tear are pulled together. A patch is made by cutting a piece of linen to shape and raveling the edges. This is coated with an adhesive (I use Higgins's Vegetable Glue), put down on the tear, and ironed with a warm iron till it is firmly attached. The picture is then left to dry under weights.

In repainting the injured spot, the part of the priming which is missing from the picture must be first replaced by picture putty. This can be made with commercial wall-patching plaster moistened with a little linseed oil and water. When this has set, it is sanded smooth and the retouching is done, if possible, with egg tempera, which will not darken with age as oil paint does. If oil paint is used for the retouching, it must be with as little oil as possible and considerably lighter than the adjacent tones. For a more serious tear, or if the canvas backing of the picture has deteriorated, the whole picture must be glued on a new piece of canvas—"relined," as the restorers say. The process is not particularly complicated. Paper is pasted to the front of the canvas with a paste made of starch, this to protect the picture and to hold the paint film together, and new canvas is glued onto the back and ironed till dry. But all this requires a more elaborate set of tools than one generally has on hand, and a more detailed explanation than suits a book like this. Enough to say that relining is simple enough if one has the tools and patience.

Framing is a much more difficult problem. And I am afraid it will always be a difficult one, for the frame has a complicated function to perform. It must set off the beauty of the picture; it must also define its kind and value. A frame is exactly like a suit of clothes which must serve both to enhance the comeliness of the wearer and to explain his social situation. To be well dressed, it is not enough that the clothes be becoming to the wearer and handsome in themselves. They must also be appropriate to the life the wearer is leading and the particular station he assumes in it. The proper clothes for a consular agent are not at all the proper clothes for an eminent cameraman. In the same way, a Rembrandt and a Piero della Francesca require different styles of framing, and neither style would fit a Matisse, even though all three pictures had identical market values. Good framing is like the best in tailoring, which can underline the wearer's natural style, point up his good looks, and enhance his prestige, and all without ever calling attention to itself. A visitor to a well-framed show should never be aware of frames at all. Frames are like clothes also in the way they go out of fashion. The serious artist of the 'eighties, for example, dressed as a Romantic poet with working-class sympathies, like Julien in *Louise;* in the 'nineties he dressed as an aesthete; in the 'twenties as a business executive. None of these styles would be suitable for the artist of today, who feels more sincere in the costume of a forty-niner or a flower child. In exactly the same way, the gold frame in an approximately Louis XIV style, which served for almost all nineteenth-century pictures, is quite unsuitable for pictures painted today, even with all its gold removed and its color changed. The Whistler frame, with its finely grooved half rounds of wood gilded in pale matte gold, is even more unsuitable. So also are the frames we found so handsome in the 'forties made from unpainted, worm-eaten chestnut. And the frames designed for pictures which I painted only a decade ago are already so out-moded that if the pictures were exhibited today, the frames would have to be changed.

What exactly constitutes the contemporary framing style is difficult to define. One knows, however, that a terser style of framing is possible than in the past. This comes partly from the example set by the Italian museums, where the ceremonious gilt mouldings which formerly announced each masterpiece have now been replaced by narrow bands of gold around the picture, and a rectangle of brocade or velvet put behind it. It is also because we have come to expect nothing more elaborate than a tiny stripping around one of the large contemporary abstractions. In both cases, it is a question of fairly large pictures. In a big picture, the edges of the canvas are much farther away from the center of interest than in a small work, farther away also from the spectator and attract his eye less strongly and consequently need less weight of frame to soften them and hold them in. In the case of a really big picture, big enough to cover most of the wall it hangs on, the picture becomes a part of the wall and needs only frame enough to make a smooth transition between the two different kinds of surface.

A small picture will not ordinarily accept this economical solution. A small picture needs a comparatively massive frame, something which concentrates the spectator's attention on the picture, shunts it away from the wall where the picture hangs, and serves to underline the picture's value as a precious object. A middle-sized picture is usually the most difficult to know what to do with. Here, the size of the detail in the moulding, the scale of carving if there is any, and the width of the inset, all must be chosen to accord with the size of detail in the picture itself. Above all, the frame must not be too heavy. A skimpy frame will rob the work of its due importance. But a frame too massive will reduce even a large picture to a picture postcard.

Contrary to what one might think, it is not necessarily the width of a frame which gives it weight. Its weight comes rather from its amount of surface area. If one measures the surface of a picture moulding, following the ins and outs of its profile from the inner edge, next to the picture, to the outer edge, where it undercuts and turns to face the wall, one gets a good indication of the frame's effective weight. This is why a narrow but deep frame is usually heavier than a broad and shallow one; why a carved frame is always more massive than an uncarved one; and why a frame whose outer face goes straight back to the wall like the side of a box is always awkwardly heavy, and why such a frame can be considerably lightened by beveling off a small strip from the back outside edges, edges one thinks are completely hidden from the spectator and without any possible effect on him.

A good frame profile is one of the most difficult things to find, as every painter knows, and every householder too who has ever tried to find among a framer's samples something not too unbecoming to a picture. Consequently, when a painter has to get his pictures framed, he is frequently driven to do it himself. He will design a moulding after some classical model, get the moulding routed into shape, cut into sizes, and made into frames by a cabinetmaker, and then he will undertake to do the finishing himself. This is tedious work but not particularly difficult. The usual base for such a finish is metal leaf. To lay the leaf, the surface of the frame must first be sanded smooth, given coats of priming or gesso to fill up the grain, and then sanded smooth again. It is then painted brick red with a lacquer paint or with watercolor which is then protected by shellac. On top of this, a coat of gold size is applied. Gold size is a fast-drying varnish to which the metal leaf will stick. When the size has dried till it is scarcely tacky any more, the metal leaf is laid down. The leaf, called dutch metal, is of brass or aluminum rolled into sheets, thin but not nearly as thin as gold leaf. The leaf is pressed into the almost-dry size with a piece of cotton or soft paper and the superfluous leaf brushed off. If the size was properly dry when it was laid, it can be burnished and will shine like metal. Brass leaf must be protected with a coat of shellac; otherwise it will tarnish and turn black. Aluminum leaf does not tarnish and needs no such protection. It has a cold, bright, leaden tone, much uglier than real silver leaf, and quite unpleasant. But it can be toned with colored shellac glazes into very useful shades of gold, from a pale, silvery gold to a heavy, dirty one.

217

Once the frame has been gilded, its tone must be adjusted to fit the picture. This involves a certain amount of rough treatment. Part of the metal is scraped off to show the red of the base. It can be given a dusty patina with thin water-color—yellow ocher and white for a warm tone and raw umber and white for a cold one, dirtied and darkened with oil and shellac glazes, and toned with black and brown shoe polish. It can be waxed and then dusted with rottenstone or talcum powder, speckled with artificial flyspecks, beaten with chains, burned with a hot poker, and shot with wormholes to give what the decorating trade calls a "distressed finish." And as long as a tiny gleam of metal still shows through, the frame will tell as gold. Such a patina is easier to apply to a carved or patterned surface than to a flat one. If the frame has flat panels, they are usually not gilded but left as panels of color, sometimes enriched with tooled designs, and some-times even marbleized.

A gold frame such as this works best on a dark picture, or at any rate, on a picture with a dark background ,which the dark gold of the frame will pick up and continue. If the tone of the picture is light, as are most pictures today, the picture will probably need a liner to separate it from the moulding, a neutral inset which eases over the abrupt change from gold to painted surface and keeps the picture from appearing crowded in and choked by its encirclement. Liners can be white, gray, or in color, in flat paint, natural wood, velvet, or raw linen, anything at all as long as the tone is becoming to the picture and neutral enough not to distract the eye. Liners can be narrow or wide, shallow or deep, beveled or flat or concave. The profile of the inset determines its weight. A flat inset gives little extra weight to a moulding; a retreating inset gives a great deal. A shadow box, which is one of the heaviest frames there is, is simply a wide liner set in a deep and narrow moulding. The width of the liner needed by a frame depends on the size or the details in the picture, and on the amount of separation re-quired between the picture and the frame. With proper adjustment of the weight and width and finish of the liner to the width and finish of the surrounding frame, almost any picture can be becomingly set off, and with the help of the proper liner, even an apparently unsuitable moulding can often be made to do, as long as it was not too heavy to begin with.

Now that the problems of framing have been so carefully elucidated, let me hope that the reader will have better luck with them than I have. For, despite all this display of knowledge and all these elaborate theoretical considerations, I myself have never succeeded in framing my own pictures. Framing a picture becomingly depends on knowing precisely what sort of picture it is, what is its character, its import, its value, and where it fits into the history of art—all of which are things very difficult for a painter to know about his own work.

All this sounds very discouraging, and indeed it is. Of the painter's three most common causes for anxiety—money, love, and framing—it is framing which will soonest drive him to a nervous breakdown. In his uncertainty, he dreams of specialists in taste, geniuses at framing, decorators who respect and understand painting, and who will know, as he does not, what are the right frames for his pictures. But even if such experts could be found and were willing, both of which are scarcely probable, they still could do little for him. The picture which framers and collectors and decorators frame so well are only those which have been successfully framed before, pictures whose character and value are known, and whose appropriate style of framing has already been established. With brand-new pictures, the experts are much less knowledgeable, and the painter is left with no way but trial and error to find out how to dress his pictures. Nevertheless, the proper kind of framing must be found. It is a necessary step in the process of evaluating the work and finding a public for it. And as we all know, nudity either as a style of dress or style of framing, however becoming it may be to young bodies on a beach or to fresh-painted pictures in the studio, has not yet become the accepted norm for public exhibition.

· 13 ·

THE PICTURE MARKET

THE FIRST WORK of mine to be sold, I seem to remember, was one of the watercolors from Cape Cod, I did while still at Harvard and bought, I think, by one of the faculty. The next was a red-chalk drawing, commissioned by the philosophy department, of Alfred North Whitehead, who in 1925 was giving a course of lectures there. Both he and Mrs. Whitehead seemed to be pleased with it, although Whitehead remarked gently that I had made him look like a Negro. Then there was another portrait commission, someone's baby granddaughter from Brookline, and I do not recall any more pictures being sold until the still life whose purchase by my generous doctor friend enabled me to stop working for mural painters and go back to France to take up my own painting again. Before this, while I was still working as a mural painter's assistant in New York, I had shown the few pictures I had to a picture merchant, hoping to be offered a show, or at least to be taken on by his gallery. He liked the paintings,

---

221

but explained that he could do nothing about them because I was occupied by another job, and there was no immediate likelihood of my painting any more. And I began to understand that the lauching of a painter by a picture merchant cannot be undertaken on the strength of one or two pictures, no matter how good they are, but on the possibility of a suite of works all done in a recognizable style. This is what I had had in my first show of red-chalk drawings in Boston—a series of drawings all done in the same scale and manner. Later, in Paris, when I was painting still life and visibly working at it every day, I had no trouble at all in getting shows; the pictures were all in a recognizable style. All had the same kind of subject matter, the same technical approach, and all were based on the same generating idea. A painter looks at his work from the inside and sees it as a series of separate pictures, each one completely different; even those which derive from the same idea, because he knows that each one presents a different aspect or further development of it. Otherwise he would not have bothered to paint them. The picture merchant, on the other hand, looks at the pictures as kindred examples of a style which the public may be taught to identify. He is more attracted by uniformity than by variety, for he knows that a recognizable style will sell itself, that painters like Corot and Canaletto, Miró, Chagall, and Bernard Buffet would not have enjoyed their spectacular commercial successes had their work not been so unmistakably typed.

Such wide distribution as this, however, is possible only in an international market. For a painter with only a local market, whose work is known in a city like New York or London or Paris and unknown elsewhere, the number of possible clients for pictures all of the same style is much more limited. This is the commercial reason, though it is not necessarily the artistic one, why a painter's successive shows must each be different, though not so different that they could not all be recognized as the same painter's work. And this is the reason why Picasso, in the early part of his career, when he was first making his way in Paris and before his international reputation became as firmly established as it is today, was led to change his style of painting so often and so radically.

Paris, when I was there, was still the undisputed center of the international market. In fact, the work of the painters living there made up the product that the international picture market sold. And even I, though I was fairly new there and showed at quite unimportant galleries, had a certain small access to the international market simply because I lived in Paris. Alfred Barr, then director of the Museum of Modern Art of New York, turned up each spring to find out what was going on and to buy for his board members, and through him, and through other visitors like Mrs. Goodspeed and Russell Hitchcock, a number of my pictures got into collections they probably would not have reached had I not been Paris-based.

My going back to America after the war had started changed this situation. Julien Levy's gallery, where I had my first serious American show, was the principal outpost in America of the advanced international market. Julien had been the first to bring here the work of the Neoromantic painters Tchelitchew and the Berman brothers, as well as such Surrealists as Dali, Max Ernst, and Yves Tanguy. (Dali and Tchelitchew did not stay with Julien long. As his wife, Joella, once explained to me, Julien could not actually believe that a picture could be worth more than seven hundred dollars, and when his painters had begun to reach such prices, they would always leave him and go to another gallery.) All these painters had established European reputations. I, on the other hand, had not been in Paris long enough to have a European market which could survive my absence, and now I was left with only a New York one.

A local market such as this is actually what most painters have, even painters who are locally very celebrated. Take for example the watercolorist Dodge MacKnight. At the time I was at Harvard, he was the best-known painter in Boston, and his annual one-man show was always bought out before the opening and at very good prices indeed. In New York, he was completely unknown. The American still-life painter Harnett offers another example of the limited area covered by a local reputation. Harnett was so well known in his time and sold so well to a provincial American public that he engendered a whole school of imitators, all painting the same sort of trompe l'oeil still lifes in the same meticulous, detailed manner, each trying his hand with varying degrees of success at Harnett's most ambitious subject—a barn door hung with guns and game, and called *After the Hunt* (Fig. 57). Harnett's public was local in that it was made up of ordinary, not particularly cultivated people who were excited by Harnett's skill in what was already an old-fashioned style. It had no connection with the informed, up-to-date public, which was the public of his contemporary, William M. Chase. Chase, though American, painted in an internationally admired style —of Manet, Sargent, Sorolla, and the rest of the late nineteenth-century virtuoso figure painters. Chase was quickly assigned his place in the history of art and got into all the books. Harnett, who had only a local market and no publicity except by word of mouth, has remained unknown to the general public until quite recently.

Word of mouth is the prime characteristic of a local market. The local

Fig. 57. WILLIAM MICHAEL HARNETT, After the Hunt, Still Life, 1883. Oil on
canvas. *The Columbus Gallery of Fine Arts, Columbus, Ohio.
Gift of Francis G. Sessions.*

painter's pictures can be known only in his particular area. There is no effective press that will take them out of it. They can be seen only at the painter's studio, at his local exhibitions, and on his clients' walls. And since the estimated value of a picture is exactly proportionate to how widely the painter's name is known, the pictures of a painter working for a local market cannot attain high prices, unless by some happy combination of circumstances, his market ceases to be local and he achieves a national reputation.

The painter wtih a national reputation, however, seldom has started off alone. He will generally be a member of a well-characterized group—the Ash Can School, for example—whose work is all based on the same approach, who have known one another at school, who put on group shows and publish manifestos and work together for their mutual interest. Behind such a nationally known group, one usually finds some astute picture merchant who knows how to put his painters in all the big national exhibitions and how to get publicity for them in the nationally circulated magazines. Mr. George Price, of the Ferragil Gallery, who launched the group of Midwestern regional painters—Curry, Benton, and Grant Wood—acted in this capacity. Alfred Stieglitz did the same, devising effective methods of promotion for his American stable of O'Keeffe, Marin, Dove, and the others, painters who worked together as a united group trying to oppose their own American homegrown form of Abstractionism to the imported European product. Nationally known painters sell for higher prices and their private clients are more numerous. Museums throughout the country also buy them, for they know that the public has read about these painters in the periodicals and are curious to see the works. The national painters usually remain severely national—Bellows and Speicher are unknown in London, and Matthew Smith and Christopher Wood, famous in London, are unknown in Paris and New York—nor can they arrive at international distribution unless the aesthetic of their work happens to fit in with the particular aesthetic which the international market is then selling. Thus, our New York group of Abstract Expressionists, Jackson Pollock, William de Kooning, and the others, started off with only national advertising. But they were able to attain international celebrity and distribution and to raise their prices from the national to the international level because they had been able to add a sort of American free-wheeling style and a small, real novelty—that of excessive canvas size—to an already established international aesthetic.

As one knows, this contemporary international style originated in Paris in the early years of our century. Impressionism, the preceding international style which our modern style replaced, also originated in Paris. On the other hand, the international style which had been prevalent before Impressionism—a school of academic anecdotal painting—had nothing particularly French about it (though it was well exemplified in the French official painting which Cézanne so bitterly described as the Salon of Monsieur Bouguereau), and art students did not necessarily have to go to France to learn to do it. Munich was much more famous for teaching painting, Rome for teaching sculpture, and it was the art schools of Munich, not Paris, which had furnished the American painters with the technical background for the landscapes of the Hudson River School, for genre scenes like those of Bingham, and for the meticulous still lifes of Peto and Harnett. However, sometime during the Second Empire, under Louis Napoleon and the Empress Eugénie, the fashion changed. Americans and everybody else began to go to Paris to study art, and American and European patrons bought their pictures there—works of Horace Vernet, Bouguereau, Corot, Meissonier, Diaz, pictures from the annual Paris Salons, and works by Impressionists. Later, after the turn of the century when modern art appeared, Paris was its natural point of distribution. And even though very few of its founders were in fact French, Paris was nevertheless the place where all the young modern painters were living.

Young modern art was vigorous, inventive, and incomprehensible. Its incomprehensibility demanded exegesis. Writers and poets have always been attracted by literary painting—Huysmans by Gustave Moreau, for example, and Ruskin by the Pre–Raphaelites (though it is true that Ruskin was even more eloquent on Turner, who to our eyes is not literary at all); and the very incomprehensibility of the modern work was itself a fascinating literary subject for them. The young poets—Apollinaire, Max Jacob, Gertrude Stein, and later Jean Cocteau—took up the movement as a cause and were such excellent polemicists that by 1914 Cubism, in particular, and modern art, in general, had gained worldwide celebrity, with major and tumultuous exhibitions in all the major capitals, and Picasso and Picabia, inseparably coupled by a fortuitous assonance, had become household words in most of Europe and America.

The enormous vigor of the movement derived from its subject matter, which was completely new. The subject matter of all previous European painting had been based on nature, was some sort of depiction or interpretation of it. The new painting avoided any imitation of nature and turned for subject matter to art itself. It was, in fact, a sort of Mannerism. Just as the Italian Mannerists of the late sixteenth century had exploited and combined the individual manners of Raphael, Michelangelo, and Leonardo, the modern painters in their turn took as subject for their pictures the analysis of some particular painting style or means of composition. The new subject first appeared in Picasso's African pictures, in which he characterized and exploited the stylistic peculiarities of some Gabon masks—African sculpture was then new to Europe. Its next development was Cubism—perhaps the style's greatest achievement—where it was used to dissect the European conventions of pictorial perspective. Here Braque and Picasso elaborated a device of perspective which Cézanne had used for composing his still lifes, a complicated form of perspective which made use of multiple points of view, and they carried it as far as it would go. Here in Cubism, the objects in the picture were reduced to their bare essentials, sometimes even to a name, so that they could be shown from several sides at once and two objects could be made to occupy the same place on the canvas. This early strict form of Cubism with its beautiful restrained tones of gray and tan lasted only a very short time; perhaps it was too strenuous a discipline to continue. But all the young moderns tried their hand at it, and its characteristic broken straight lines and semicircles became the trademark of the movement. Leaving Cubism, the movement divided and went in two different directions. One branch, the pure Abstractionists, proceeded to examine the abstract elements which make up a picture—shapes, color contrasts, and devices for composition. The other branch, to which Picasso himself belonged, elaborated on Picasso's African experiment and went on to explore and to abstract the basic elements of other unfamiliar and exotic pictorial styles. The pure Abstractionists, like Mondrian and the Dutch De Stijl school, avoided all imagery whatever. The Parisian contingent, Braque, Picasso, and the others, believed with Gertrude Stein that a completely abstract work will necessarily be either a meaningless decoration or obscene, and always built their pictures around some subject, even though it might not be apparent in the finished work what the subject was.

All the modern painters, however, agreed in insisting that a picture was not a window to be looked through; that it was an object complete in itself. Thus, in order to banish all illusion of depth from a picture and to emphasize the tangible reality of the picture surface, they plastered it with all sort of unpictorial things like clippings from newspapers, grainings to imitate false wood, or cigarette wrappers. The Dadaists went on from this to construct their work entirely out of such accidental materials, insisting that all forms of art were equally valid and equally valueless, and that it made no difference at all what they were made from.

The modern movement was so vigorous and so full of fascinating possibilities that it immediately spread all over Europe to be tried out everywhere. It reached America in 1913, only a decade after its inception, and also caused a major revolution here. So rapid had been its development that by the time the First World War had begun, most of the inventions and devices that make up the repertory of the International School today had already been discovered and exploited, the possible styles had been established, the reputations of the great painters made, and their most famous pictures painted. After the war, with poets and publicists and picture dealers working and writing to support the movement, modern art became firmly established as the painting of our time. The Museum of Modern Art of New York was founded to conserve and show it, and this was followed by similar museums in most of the major cities. Instruction in modern-style painting began to crowd out the more conservative forms of art instruction from the American painting academies and succeeded in banishing them completely from the American universities, which then proceeded to take over the teaching of painting. The great international shows like the Venice Biennale, the São Paulo Biennale, and even the Carnegie International in Pittsburgh, turned into exhibitions of exclusively modern-art-style pictures. Each country, even very minor ones, developed its own schools of modern painting especially for these shows, sending in large and striking pictures specifically constructed to be shown at international exhibitions of abstract art. The Whitney Museum of New York, which devotes itself to American painting, is now no different from any of the international exhibitions except that the international-style pictures it shows are all by Americans. The art magazines refuse all honor to painters working in another style. The figurative painters, here and in Paris and in London, still go on painting and lead productive and by no means unhappy lives. They have their dealers who believe in them and sell their pictures, and their devoted clients who buy them, but all this in a strictly local market. There are, of course, a few exceptions like Norman Rockwell or Andrew Wyeth, who are indeed figurative painters and nevertheless have achieved a national distribution. This, however, is not from their qualities as painters, which are very great, but for their ability to tell a touching story.

Actually, the national markets for painting have almost disappeared; what little is left has merged with the international one. And if a painter is to be placed on the international market, he must have some connection with the contemporary international style. Consequently, pictures by figurative painters are unlikely to be accepted by the juries of either national or international shows, even when the jury is composed of painters. Figurative painting has so bad a press that no artist-juryman wishes to compromise himself by a vote that might indicate conservative leanings. It is also unlikely that a figurative painter would be taken on the staff of a university where only the international style is being taught. And surprisingly enough, this firm establishment of the modern style has been achieved in the face of an intense and unceasing public resistance. This is exactly the contrary to French official nineteenth-century salon painting, whose firm establishment was maintained by the French public's complete devotion to the sentimental and anecdotal subject matter of the salon painters.

The firm establishment the international style enjoys today, however, does not mean that all international-style painters sell their work well. Unless they have been successfully launched, they sell very badly indeed. Launching a painter means transferring him from a local market to a national market and, if possible, to an international one. This is a troublesome and complex affair and is not undertaken unless somebody expects to make a great deal of money by doing so. The painter himself has seldom the talent for public relations, which the operation requires. (Remember how Gauguin, on his return from Tahiti, dressed himself up in fancy clothes and carried a parakeet on his shoulder in an effort to publicize his Tahitian pictures, and how miserably he failed at it.) Besides, the painter is usually unwilling to take that much time from his work. Launching a painter is a job for specialists. It is usually undertaken by a merchant or by a group of merchants, or by a vigorous and ambitious wife. There must be available for sale a sizable body of work done in a consistent manner. Launching a painter is easier if he belongs to a group of painters all working in the same style, and easier still if the group has literary friends to help it along, to write books about it and articles in the avant-garde intellectual magazines. Coverage in magazines of large circulation, like *Time* or *Life* or *Paris Match,* may do more harm than good. Investors and collectors will listen to a small ingroup which is thought to be in touch with advanced ideas and likely to know which way the market will go. But acclaim in the popular press for a new painter will not persuade anyone to buy him, while wide acclaim for an established painter informs the serious collectors merely that his prices have now gone very high. On the other hand, a wide public acclaim that is also accompanied by the approval of an ingroup, will serve to sell his pictures to people like directors of great corporations, who are not necessarily interested in the pictures themselves, but who can use the intellectual prestige and impressive money value of the pictures as a means of conspicuous display. A double acclaim like this will also sell to museums, for the directors know that pictures which have appeared so largely in the news will attract new visitors. Pop Art, as I have pointed out, seems to be directly designed for museum purchase. For the works are in general too emphatic and cumbersome for private homes and too sardonic for a director's office.

The poet and master press agent Jean Cocteau acted as ingroup friend for the modern movement in the years of its great expansion after the first war. André Breton, the poet who had organized the remains of the Dada group into the Surrealist Movement, was an even better adviser and press agent for his own poets and painters. He had an extraordinary sense of how to create a scandal and how to make use of it, and to this end wrote incendiary manifestos, engaged in violent public aesthetic and literary quarrels, organized expositions with overtones of sex and cruelty ingeniously planned in advance to scandalize the public, and tyrannically imposed a unity of purpose on his group and a code of scandalous behavior on its members. The painter Salvador Dali, who as a young man belonged to the Surrealist group, probably acquired his mastery of this kind of publicity from Breton, though Dali's means have always been cruder and on a much lower intellectual level. During the war, Breton left France to seek refuge in New York, where he was already celebrated in advanced painting and literary circles, and where as a matter of course he must have encountered the group of young Abstract Expressionists. If the international acceptance these painters acquired shortly afterward was not implemented by Breton himself, then the example of the Surrealists at least showed them how to do it. The American Beatniks, an only moderately interesting literary movement, got a great deal more celebrity than their talents warranted by techniques of public scandal on the Surrealist model. The Pop Artists also work as a group and exploit a form of scandal perhaps more akin to Dada's genial nonsense than to Surrealism's moralistic fervor. One remembers that Andy Warhol, the most prominent member of the American group, began as a crack advertising artist and one of the best layout men on Madison Avenue. Indeed, expert professional publicity is now so important in picture marketing that the standard form of contract between painter and dealer has been changed by it. Formerly one third of the price paid for a picture went to the dealer, two thirds to the painter, and the incidental expenses of framing and publicity were more or less shared between them. Today in Paris, I am told, one third goes to the dealer, one third to the painter, and one third to the publicity man who knows how to advance the painter's fame and prices.

The general public is always astonished at these prices. It does not understand that there are two quite different sorts of picture buying, each with its own scale of prices; one is a consumer's market, the other a market in futures. Prices in both markets depend on the quality of the picture and on how well the painter's name is known. In the consumer's market, the picture is bought because the buyer likes it, and bought not as an investment but to keep. The price is reasonably low and is paid by the buyer out of his income, not out of his capital. If it is an old picture, it will be an unsigned one or by an unknown or obscure painter, and will have no other value besides its own pictorial qualities. If it is a new picture, it will be the work of a painter painting for a local, or at most, a national market. Pictures which have reached the international market are already too expensive to be paid for out of income or to think of as consumer goods.

The other market, a market for futures, is for investors. Pictures here are bought not necessarily for the pleasure of having them on the wall, though this is certainly an important consideration, but with the hope of eventually making a profitable resale. The solid conservative values in this market are in old masters, and among the old masters, the second-string pictures of a great painter will usually prove a sounder investment than a celebrated masterpiece. A masterpiece requires a princely establishment for its display, a condition which limits the possibility of a quick resale. The wildcat, speculative values in this market are in modern and contemporary works. Here, the buyer hopes to emulate the fabulously successful collectors of the early part of our century who got in on the ground floor, collectors who bought pictures that everyone else found incomprehensible, at cheap prices, from painters who were poor or even starving and generally considered mad, collectors like Barnes, for example, whose pictures were laughed at by all Philadelphia; Gertrude Stein, who did her collecting on so small a budget that when she acquired a Ford, she had to stop buying pictures because the expense of running the car took all available cash; or Mrs. Havemeyer, who when in later years was asked how she came to think of buying Impressionists, answered that her family were poor people and could not afford a Meissonier. It must be remembered, however, that such collectors usually had an artist around to guide them. Dr. Barnes had the painter Glackens as an intimate friend. The Steins and the Cone sisters were friends of Picasso, Matisse, Juan Gris, and all the others. And the Havemeyers had Mary Cassatt, a family connection from Philadelphia. Very few collectors have such advantages. Most of them must rely on knowing picture merchants and trying to find out from them what trends of painting will next be pushed and which young painter launched.

These speculative values are based on a piece of folklore which the successes of the collectors earlier in our century seem to substantiate, and which even serious museum people are inclined to credit. It is, in fact, quite currently taken for granted that pictures which a subsequent time will hail as works of genius are all done by mad, misunderstood, and starving artists, and that these pictures can be had quite cheap if one gets there in time. And even if the prices are by now already high, the fact that the works are incomprehensible will make them rise still more.

None of this is entirely true. To begin with, painters of talent have seldom starved. The indigent young artists in Murger's *Scènes de la Vie de Bohème,* whose example seems to assert the contrary, were not young painters of genius; they were only the picturesque young hippies of the time. The Impressionists as young men were certainly poor. But the more famous of them ended with comfortable fortunes and even the obscurer ones did not starve. The Post-Impressionists had a much harder time of it. Cézanne himself was well-off, much better off than he is shown in his role as hero of Zola's novel *L'Oeuvre,* nor did he commit suicide in despair, as Zola made him do. Still, it was not till the end of his life that he had the slightest recognition. Van Gogh and Gauguin, on the other hand, were indeed desperately poor. Van Gogh had a picture-dealer brother who kept him going. Gauguin had no money and no success and died in extreme poverty. None of the three was able to sell his pictures, probably, I should imagine because the pictures were not radical enough. There was an enormous difference in style between Impressionist painting and the Salon pictures. But between Impressionism and Post-Impressionism there was much less difference, probably not enough to attract the confirmed collectors of Impressionism, to whom Post-Impressionism must have seemed only a minor variant of the same themes. The next wave after the Post-Impressionists, the Nabis Bonnard and Vuillard, sold well from the beginning. None of the modern artists starved either, though Modigliani died early from dissipation. The young Picasso called attention to his bohemianism by dressing in sweaters instead of jacket and tie. But they were the most expensive imported sweaters, bought at Old England on the boulevard.

So much for the legend of the starving artist. As for the other part of it—the notion that good artists, if not actually all mad, are at any rate always misunderstood—one of the earliest and clearest statements of this is in Gertrude Stein's *Composition as Explanation,* a collection of the lectures she delivered in Oxford to the Ordinary Society in 1926. The idea is briefly this: An artist of genius has the ability to see the present, to see things as they actually are now today, whereas the rest of us can see only the past; instead of seeing the things we have now before our eyes, we see only our memory of them. Thus we are led to interpret the world we live in according to conceptions which are actually out-of-date. The work of an artist of genius, on the other hand, presents a view of the world as it is at the time the artist is painting it. This view no one else has yet seen, and there will inevitably be a certain lag of time before it can be seen and understood by the rest of the world. Consequently, the inevitable penalty of genius in a painter is that he is not understood by his contemporaries.

All this is more or less true. As Proust pointed out, a work of art creates its own public, and not until this public has come into existence can the work receive its due acclaim. But nevertheless, even though a genius may not be understood by his contemporaries, it does not follow that all incomprehensible works are works of genius. There are far too many such around today to accord this honor to them all. Modern art itself was basically esoteric, and the international style which continues its traditions is so consistently arcane that incomprehensibility has now become the characteristic trademark of a style and not a proof of excellence.

Since the value of a new work can no longer be inferred from its incomprehensibility alone, a simpler criterion, that of novelty has been adopted to supplement it. Besides being easy to recognize and catalog, the novelty of a work is supposed to give a reliable clue to its future worth since, according to the currently accepted ideas of art history, artistic advance has always been the prerogative of the Left, and solid and lasting artistic values are to be found only in the novel and unconventional works of revolutionaries. Thus, by this theory, the painting of David is much finer than the painting of Ingres, and Delacroix's is finer than either, though this last is very doubtful. I suspect that Delacroix is thought of as a fine colorist, not because of the color in his pictures, which to us today does not seem particularly subtle or brilliant, but because he wrote so enchantingly on the subject. Thus also, Courbet the Communard painted better pictures than any of Corot's, except perhaps Corot's earliest. All this, of course, is more than questionable. But it is not questionable in the least that all we admire today in the painting of the last hundred years was the work of an underground and not an establishment. Manet and Courbet shocked their contemporaries by the new brutality of their technique and the brashness of their subjects. The Impressionists were an underground, as were the Post-Impressionists, and all were opposed by the official salons. Even Degas, who as a pupil of Ingres was the finest academic painter of his century, was classed by the Salon as a Leftist for making use of the leftist Impressionist techniques. Modern art itself began as an underground. And though it has changed and risen to become the official establishment in control of exhibitions, publicity, and art education, it still looks on itself as an underground movement and has adopted novelty as its most insistent characteristic. "Who was the first to do it" has taken on prime importance in contemporary art history, the first to paint white on white, the first to use Plexiglas in sculpture. Even the first painter who thought to exhibit a blank canvas slashed with razor blades (Lucio Fontana) or painted his figure piece by pouring paint on the model and rolling her on the canvas (Yves Klein) have their established values and their names in the history books, though one might consider these particular novelties funnier as stories than useful as means of expression, and scarcely arcane at all. Just the same, if a painter's work is to be included in the international exhibitions and priced on the international market, it must be, if possible, esoteric, and, even more important, it must be novel.

The sums paid for pictures by well-publicized painters on the international market are almost unbelievable. A detail in the American tax laws has up to now done something to help this along. A gift to a museum counts as a gift to a charitable institution, and the value of the picture given to a museum can be deducted from the donor's income to place him in a lower income bracket. The picture, however, must be one the museum is willing to accept. It must also be expensive enough to make the troublesome operation worthwhile, that is to say, priced at least around the twenty-thousand-dollar level. An authentic old master of museum quality in that price range is hard to come upon. Witness the collection of old masters purchased for the São Paulo Museum some ten years ago and put on exhibit here. Few of them were first-rate pictures; nevertheless, they were the best that could be got together nowadays on a large but not unlimited budget. But on the other hand, there are plenty of highly publicized living painters whose work the museum would be delighted to own and whose prices can be adjusted to attain the necessary level. This practice is so widespread today that a young painter cannot claim to have really arrived until he has sold his twenty-thousand-dollar picture. Where he has arrived, of course, is in the upper brackets of the international market, for no local or national market could pay such prices for a living painter.

The prices of pictures which have reached the international market are indeed fantastic, so out of scale with picture prices on a local market that one is driven to ask how long they can be maintained. One knows that the painter's death, and the next change of taste, will both certainly affect them. The prices of a painter who has been highly publicized during his lifetime are likely to go down after his death. Sargent, Meissonier, Bouguereau, today bring nothing like what the pictures were worth when the painters were alive and at the height of their fame, though they still keep better prices than is generally imagined. Pictures by the once celebrated master of a school, even if out of fashion, at one time represented important investments, and there will still be dealers and collectors who are interested in keeping their prices up. On the other hand, the less well-known members of the school are easily forgotten and their prices sink to nothing, or to the usual prices paid on a local market for an unknown painter. What a salon-style picture by an unknown follower of Bouguereau would bring today, no matter how well painted, would depend on the skill of the merchant and the fantasy of the buyer. Just the same, if there happened to turn up a string of works, all in an easily recognizable individual style, by one of these dead and unknown painters, the painter can then be rediscovered and his name added to the list of profitable investments. But even then, both for the well-known painters of a past establishment, and for the rediscovered ones, the prices of their pictures can never be maintained in face of one of the radical changes of taste which periodically occur in the world of art. After such a change, the ideas on which the works are based become boring and unacceptable to everyone. At this point, the market for everything connected with the unfashionable ideas ceases to exist, even the provincial market. How fast the prices fall depends on how radical is the change of taste and how long the establishment can resist the attacks of the hostile underground which has brought on the change.

I suspect that such a change of taste is about to happen. It is not that any organized hostile underground has yet appeared; it is rather that the ideas on which the present establishment is based, ideas once vigorous and inspiring, are now more than two generations old and have grown trite and tiresome with repetition. It is generally known and everywhere accepted that what one calls modern music is all derived from material invented before 1914 by the modern composers Debussy, Satie, Stravinsky, and Schönberg. But one does not realize that if the crucial date is taken as 1918, exactly the same sort of thing is true of modern art. All of its methods and tenets were invented and perfected before the First World War ended. The only real novelty that came later was Dada, from noncombatant Switzerland, where artists and writers were not being mobilized. After the war, there was considerable expansion and consolidation in modern art just as in modern music, but nothing was added that was radically new. Even apparently new developments like Neoromanticism and Surrealism and even Op Art and Pop Art are only old materials given a new twist. The Neoromantic pictures of Bérard and Tchelitchew use the subjects and sentiments that Picasso had

235

already treated in his youth. Surrealism took over Dada's somewhat childish anarchism to turn it to subversive ends with shock material derived from Freud and Trotsky. Op Art is only a more elaborate form of pure Abstractionism. And Pop Art, the latest and most successful novelty of the international style, is only Dada redone in supermarket packaging. Each repetition and restatement has taken away from the vigor and shock value of the original ideas. The steady weakening of these basic conceptions was well illustrated in the retrospective exhibition of Picasso's sculpture recently shown at the Museum of Modern Art of New York, an exhibition which begins with imposing works, still today shocking, fascinating, and impenetrable, to end in charming and frivolous fooleries and parlor games.

Dada itself was an antiart movement directed toward the destruction of all artistic values. Now one is faced with the curious paradox that the latest in official art today is a form of Dadaism, and thus an antiart. Consequently, if an underground is to exist, it must take the form of an anti-antiart, and inevitably present the appearance of a return to traditional artistic values. By the establishment's own theory of artistic progress, the only valid artistic evolution is one which by its very nature is inacceptable to the current establishment. And one is driven to the strange conclusion that the most advanced and revolutionary thing in the art world today would be simple representational painting.

Tactically speaking, however, representational painting would not make up into a very effective underground. It would have too much trouble finding capable young recruits. The techniques of figurative painting are complex and difficult. They were already badly taught when I went to school some fifty years ago, and the traditions were already getting lost. Today it is almost impossible to find out anything about them. No one knows any longer how painters like Meissonier got their effects; there is probably no one alive who could make a copy in true color and exact detail of Gérôme's *Moorish Bath,* which hangs in the Boston Fine Arts Museum (Fig. 58). Whether or not one likes the picture, it would be good to be able to handle paints so competently; Degas, at any rate, could. But where one would go today to learn to do it, I would not know; I would not know even where to go to find competent instruction in painting from nature. I am afraid that the youngsters of today who wish to learn such things will have to find them out all by themselves. Most certainly they cannot learn them from books. Skills like drawing from life or playing the piano or driving a car, skills which depend on an elaborate training of eye or ear or hand, can be taught only by a live and present teacher who can show the student how the